AMERICAN
POETRY

Also by Robert Bly

POETRY

Silence in the Snowy Fields
The Light Around the Body
The Teeth Mother Naked at Last
Jumping Out of Bed
Sleepers Joining Hands
Old Man Rubbing His Eyes
The Morning Glory
This Body Is Made of Camphor and Gopherwood
This Tree Will Be Here for a Thousand Years
The Man in the Black Coat Turns
Loving a Woman in Two Worlds
Selected Poems

TRANSLATIONS (POETRY)

Twenty Poems of Georg Trakl
(with James Wright)
Neruda and Vallejo: Selected Poems
(with James Wright and John Knoepfle)
Lorca and Jimenez: Selected Poems
Friends, You Drank Some Darkness. Martinson, Ekelöf,
and Tranströmer: Selected Poems
Bashō: Twelve Poems
The Kabir Book: 44 of the Ecstatic Poems of Kabir
Twenty Poems of Rolf Jacobsen
Mirabai: Six Versions
Selected Poems of Rainer Maria Rilke

Robert Bly

AMERICAN
POETRY

Wildness and Domesticity

Harper Perennial

A Division of HarperCollinsPublishers

A hardcover edition of this book was published in 1990 by
Harper & Row, Publishers.

Copyright acknowledgments can be found on page 339.

First HarperPerennial Edition published 1991.

Designed by Barbara DuPree Knowles

THE LIBRARY OF CONGRESS HAS CATALOGUED THE HARDCOVER EDITION AS FOLLOWS:

Bly, Robert.
    American poetry : wildness and domesticity / Robert Bly.—1st ed.
        p.   cm.
    ISBN 0-06-016265-1
    1. American poetry—20th century—History and criticism.
I. Title.
PS323.5.B63   1990
811'.509—dc20   89-45628

ISBN 0-06-092082-3 (pbk.)
92 93 94 95 WBC/MB 10 9 8 7 6 5 4 3

Contents

♦ v ♦

Contents

Preface

This book gathers together essays and appreciations that I've written over the last thirty years. Part One sums up the platform or viewpoint of my magazine, *The Fifties, The Sixties, and The Seventies.* Some essays are polemical in tone, calculated to draw blood from the old King, and to suggest new ideas for writing of poetry. By the old King I mean the conservative mind-set inherited from Eliot and Pound, and the triumphant flatness inherited from Descartes and Locke. Not all the essays are fair. One-sidedness becomes elaborate in "A Wrong Turning in American Poetry," and I regret the rudeness to individual poets. However, the rudeness belongs to the moment and the historical situation in which the essays were born, and so I have left the essays mostly as they were, giving the date in each case.

Part Two of the book gathers together readings of twelve contemporary poets whom I admire or detest; in one or two essays I express both feelings about the same poet. I have left a few essays more or less as first written years ago; others, like those on Louis Simpson and James Dickey, I've put together from pieces written at different times, noted as such; and still others, like those on James Wright, Thomas McGrath, Etheridge Knight, Donald Hall, and Galway Kinnell, I have written in the last two or three years. Many other poets I admire are missing only because I haven't written about them yet.

Part Three asks in what direction American poetry has gone in the thirty years after Wallace Stevens's death. Americans have developed in the last decades a lively poetry that offers personal revelation primarily, traditional meaning less, and form least of all. If the rider is the student of images, the metrist, and the contemplator, and the horse the rhythm, we educate the rider but not the horse. I've added to these speculations an interview with Wayne Dodd that touches on university workshops and their influence.

Robert Bly

PART ONE

Looking for
Dragon Smoke

The Roads
of Association

About the old black dress of American realism that Frank
Norris and Dreiser wore, Wallace Stevens says,

> *Ach, Mutter,*
> *this old black dress,*
> *I have been embroidering*
> *French flowers on it.*

The flowers are French because the French poets were
the first as a group to adopt underground passages of
association as the major path. We hide all that by calling
them symbolists, but poet after poet through several
generations gave his entire life to exploring these paths
of association—Gérard de Nerval, Lautréamont, Aloy-
sius Bertrand, Baudelaire, and Mallarmé. We remember
Poulet as well, on whose poems Wallace Stevens mod-
eled so many of his poems in *Harmonium*. Eliot's zani-
ness entered his work through a French poet, Laforgue.
  The Spanish poets of this century—Machado, Alberti, Jiménez, Blas de Otero, Hernandez—loved the

new paths as much as the French. They considered the paths roads. Antonio Machado said,

> Why should we call
> these accidental furrows roads?
> Everyone who moves on
> walks like Jesus, on the sea.

Machado noticed that fear of sinking prevents many writers from association, or from "moving on":

> Mankind owns four things
> that are no good at sea.
> Anchor, rudder, oars,
> and the fear of going down.

Machado says,

> It doesn't matter now if the golden wine
> overflows from your crystal goblet,
> or if the sour wine dirties the pure glass . . .
>
> You know the secret corridors
> of the soul, the roads that dreams take,
> and the calm evening
> where they go to die . . .

Machado's calmness comes from the fact that he *does* know the secret roads. He will not follow the old collective tracks any longer. Confessional poetry and what is called the workshop poem represent a regression to nineteenth-century poetry. I think that backward movement is associated with the fondness of American poets for old black dresses and their determination that the black dress of life will suffice. Most of the active American poets write as if Hölderlin and Novalis had never lived, nor Poulet, whom Stevens adopted as a master. Machado, by contrast, is calm because he knows that some new depth has come to the Western mind in reverie; at least it has come to his. The change frees him from an obsession with constant publication.

> While dreaming, perhaps, the hand
> Of the man who broadcasts the starts like grain
> made the lost music start once more
> like the note from a huge harp,
> and the frail wave came to our lips
> in the form of one or two words that had some truth.

Juan Ramón Jiménez, whose poetry is a model of the wider association, invented a powerful image for the discovery of new associative depths to the mind:

> I have a feeling that my boat
> has struck, down there in the depths,
> against a great thing. And nothing
> happens! Nothing . . . Silence . . . Waves . . .
>
> Nothing happens! Or has everything happened,
> and are we standing now, quietly, in the new life?

So much of the experience of the ecstatic widening of association has been denied to us, because many of our active critics do not honor association and are ignorant of Spanish poetry. A good leap is thought of as a lucky happening; if it doesn't appear, well at least the poet "achieved what he set out to do." Our critics often stubbornly insist on preserving the old black dress without embroidery, especially if made of good American material. Some critics try to substitute Emerson for Lorca, or concentrate on "anxieties of influence." But it is possible that swift association belongs not to techniques so much as meaning. An antiwar poem, for example, with swift association, and a poem with dull association have two different meanings. Wallace Stevens, one of our prime opponents of dull association, wrote once about commencement exercises. His poem, "On the Manner of Addressing Clouds," begins,

> Gloomy grammarians in golden gowns,
> meekly you keep the mortal rendezvous,
> eliciting the still sustaining pomps
> of speech which are like music so profound,
> they seem an exaltation without sound.

The "pomps of speech," the embroideries of the old black dress, are important, if the grammarians in the drifting waste of the world are to be accompanied by more than "mute bare splendors of the sun and moon."

1972

A Wrong Turning
in American Poetry

I

American poetry resembles a group of huge spiral arms whirling about in space. Eliot and Pound are moving away at tremendous speeds. Marianne Moore and Jeffers are driving into space also. This island universe is rushing away from its own center.

Let me contrast this picture with another. Spanish poetry of this century is moving inward, concentrating. Antonio Machado stands at the center of Spanish poetry, standing at the center of himself as well. His poems are strange without being neurotic. His thought is abundant and clear, near the center of life. The younger Spanish poets can judge where they are from where he is. They can look in and see him standing there.

In American poetry, on the other hand, a young poet cannot take Pound, Eliot, or Moore for a master without severe distortion of his own personality. They whirled about so far out that anyone who follows them will freeze to death. If American poetry has a center it would seem to be William Carlos Williams. His poetry however shows a fundamental absence of spiritual intensity. He is in fact as much caught up in destructive expansion as the others.

II

Eliot, Pound, Moore, and Williams, all born within five years of each other, form a poetic generation we might call the generation of 1917. They support certain ideas with great assurance. Eliot's support of the idea of the "objective correlative" is an example. His phrasing of the idea is as follows: "The only way of expressing emotion in the form of art is by finding an 'objective correlative'; in other words, a set of objects, a situation, a chain of events which shall be the formula of that *particular* emotion." The tone is authoritative, but the statement is not true. With "objective" here, we stumble onto a word we will find over and over again in the work of the 1917 generation. These men have more trust in the objective, outer world than in the inner world. As poets, they want to concern themselves with objects. The word "formula" above suggests the desire to be scientific, to study things. Eliot says in essence that *objects* are essential in a poem. He wants to arrange them in a formula, as a scientist would, so that the controlled experiment can be repeated any number of times.

As a program, the search for the objective correlative merely obstructs poetry. What does the search for this formula result in? The impulse for the poem does not flow forward into the language. Instead the impulse is stopped: the poet searches about for the proper formula in the public world. This means working up the poem as an idea—for example, in terms of the lower classes ("Sweeney Erect") or in terms of Greek myth ("Sweeney Agonistes"). Greek myths and the lower classes are thought to be very objective. However, the impulse to the poem is broken. True freshness and surprise are impossible. The poet's eyes are not on the impulse but are constantly looking over the public world for reliable sets of objects. Finally, the poet's own mind becomes objective: he becomes the public.

Modern Spanish poetry—to continue our contrast— denies Eliot's thesis of the relevance of the objectivizing process. Ricardo Gullon, for example, has said that the purpose of poetry "is to transfer an intuition." How is an intuition to be transferred? Guillaume de Torre, the greatest contemporary Spanish critic, holds up the personal, even the intimate poem. Intuition is embodied in experiences private to the poet (which the reader can nonetheless share) "and not in common experiences from the public domain masquerading as unique and vital. T. S. Eliot's 'objective correlative' and other vulgarities dressed up in cryptic terms are nothing but so many frauds."

Lorca has a poem describing his emotions while walking on the streets of New York, feeling that he is aging, being rapidly killed by the sky. He does not talk of Circe or the clothes of bums sleeping on the sidewalk. He says,

> Among the forms which are moving toward the
>   serpent,
> And the forms which are searching for the crystal,
> I'll grow long hair.
>
> With the tree of amputated limbs which does not sing,
> And the boy child with the white face of the egg.

With all the tiny animals who have gone insane,
And the ragged water which walks on its dry feet.

Lorca conveys his emotion not by any "formula" but by means that do not occur to Eliot—by passionate spontaneity. The phrase "objective correlative" is astoundingly passionless. For Lorca there is no time to think of a cunning set of circumstances that would carry the emotion in a dehydrated form to which the reader need only add water.

Pound said in 1911, "I believe that the proper and perfect symbol is the natural object." Pound considers poetry to be fundamentally a repository of wisdom. He wishes to put into the *Cantos* as many important thoughts and conversations and fragments of the classics as he can, so that should a man be able to own only one book he could own the *Cantos* and thereby possess the truth about economics and government as well as culture. The poem is thus defined with no reference to the unconscious. Instead of the unconscious there is economics. Relations between parts of the outer world take the place of inner relations and of the inner world. The book takes what it needs by force. As a poem, the *Cantos* annexes other people's ideas, facts, other languages. The poem is like an infinitely expanding metropolis, eating up more and more of the outer world, with less and less life at the center. The personality of the poet is driven out of the poem. The expanding poem, like the expanding city, has no personality. The idea of the poem as the essence of the author's personality—Yeats believed this is what a poem was—is entirely lost. How can the personality be present if the unconscious is pushed out?

Marianne Moore's poetry also represents a treasure-house—a feminine one. The objects in the poem are fragments, annexed, and the poem is a parlor full of knickknacks carefully arranged. Melville leaves such a room and goes to sea: there he sees whales moving about in the sea their whole lives, winds thrashing freely, primitive forces that act out their own inward strength. Returning to land he becomes a revolutionary because in society he sees such elementary forces curtailed; he asks why they must be checked and lamed. The purpose of Marianne Moore's art is exactly opposite: it is to reconcile us to living with hampered forces. She brings in animals and fish, but only fragments of them—beaks of birds, single wings of dragonflies, the dorsal fin of a whale, the teeth of snakes, the forepaw of an otter—all adopted to domestic life. Everything is reduced in size, reduced to human dimensions, as in old New England parlors, where there was "a shark's backbone made into a walking stick." The poem becomes a temporary excursion into the dangerous world of nature, with an immediate and safe return already envisioned—a kind of picnic. The fragments of animals that appear are separated from their inner force, their wildness, and turned from living things into objects. A poem is conceived as an exercise in propriety.

William Carlos Williams's work reflects a similar attachment to objects. "No ideas but in things!" he said. His poems show great emotional life mingled with the drive of the intelligence to deal with outward things—but no inward life, if by inward life we mean an interest in spiritual as well as psychological intensity. Williams was a noble man, of all the poets in his generation the warmest and most human. Still, his ideas contained something destructive: there is in them a drive toward the extinction of personality. Williams's "No ideas but in things!" is a crippling program. Besides the ideas in things there are ideas in images and in feelings. True, bits of broken glass are preferable for poetry to fuzzy generalities such as virtue or patriotism. But images like Lorca's "black horses and dark people are riding over the deep roads of the guitar" also contain ideas and give birth to ideas. Williams asked poetry to confine itself to wheelbarrows, bottle caps, weeds—with the artist "limited to the range of his contact with the objective world." Keeping close to the surface becomes an obsession. The effect of Williams's thought, therefore, was to narrow the language of poetry—to narrow it to general remarks mixed with bits of glass and paper bags, with what Pound called "natural objects." Williams says, "The good poetry is where the vividness comes up true like in prose but better. That's poetry."

BETWEEN WALLS

The back wings
of the

hospital where
nothing

will grow lie
cinders

in which shine
the broken

pieces of a green
bottle

In that Williams poem, the personality and the imagination are merely two among many guests. The imagination has to exist as best it can in a poem crowded with objects. In the bare poems of some of Williams's followers the personality of the poet is diffused among lampposts and match folders, and vanishes. The poet appears in the poem only as a disembodied anger or an immovable eye.

The point in contrasting Lorca's language with Williams's is not that Lorca's poems are richer but that Lorca approaches his poetry with entirely different artistic principles—among them the absolute essentiality of the image. These ideas bear fruit in the poems. Lorca's poems have many things in them sharply observed ("black doves puttering the putrid waters"), but they also have images, also passion, wild leaps, huge arsenic lobsters falling out of the sky.

Charles Olson, about fifty, is generally considered the main transmitter of the ideas of Williams and Pound to the present generation. In Olson's prose, their outward direction is set down even more programmatically, as in "Projective Verse"—an essay that echoes T. E. Hulme—in which Olson says,

> *Objectism is the getting rid of the lyrical interference of the individual as ego, of the "subject" and his soul, that peculiar presumption by which western man has interposed himself between what he is as creature of nature (with certain instructions to carry out) and those other creations of nature which we may, with no derogation, call objects.*

In demanding that the poet get rid of himself as a subjective person Olson is simply restating Eliot's belief in the desirability of "extinguishing the personality." To Olson the poet's inwardness is "lyrical interference." Some Zen teachers use language like this, but their meaning is exactly the opposite. The aim of Zen, as of a poet like Rilke, is to make men more and more inward until they stop admiring objects, at which point they will be able to see them clearly, if they wish to.

The ideas of the 1917 generation are quite consistent. Eliot and Pound conceive maturity as a growth of outwardness. Eliot's later plays are naturally more outward than his earlier plays, the *Cantos* more outward than *Lustra*. The opposite is true of Yeats and Rilke. Rilke was more inward at thirty than at twenty; more inward at fifty than at thirty.

In this country we have a great reluctance to admit that directions can be incompatible. We want to follow both the Pound-Olson direction and the Rilke direction. Yet in *Letters to a Young Poet* Rilke writes, "Give up all that. You are looking outward, and that above all you should not do now. There is only one single way. Go into yourself." And he tells Kappus that poetry will come "from this turning inward, from this sinking into your private world." Rilke believes that the poet actually experiences the soul, does not share the mass's preoccupation with objects.

If we are to develop clear principles in our poetry we must honestly say that we cannot reconcile the inward direction of Rilke with the outward direction of the Williams-Pound-Olson movement. This is why Pound talks of Rilke so little. A man cannot turn his face at the same moment toward the inward world and the outer world: he cannot face both south and north at the same moment.

III

I have tried to point out that the 1917 generation had a rather unified set of ideas centered on objectivism—shared by all the major poets of that generation despite their other differences. All later poetry has been written, necessarily, under the influence of these ideas. Now how can we describe our poetry since the twenties in a way that will include Winters as well as Lowell, Eberhart as well as Ciardi?

It is first of all a poetry without spiritual life. The beginning of spiritual life is a horror of emptiness that our people feel every day, but it is Rilke who has described such a state, not one of us.

> Already the ripening barberries are red,
> And in their bed the aged asters hardly breathe.
> Whoever now is not rich inside, at the end of
>   summer,
> Will wait and wait, and never be himself.
>
> Whoever now is unable to close his eyes
> Absolutely certain that a crowd of faces
> Is only waiting till the night comes
> In order to stand up around him in the darkness—
> That man is worn out, like an old man.
>
> Nothing more will happen to him, no day will arrive,
> And everything that does happen will cheat him.
> Even you, my God. And you are like a stone
> Which draws him daily deeper into the depths.

Our recent poetry is also a poetry in which the poem is considered to be a construction independent of the poet. It is imagined that when the poet says "I" in a poem he does not mean himself, but rather some other person—"the poet"—a dramatic hero. The poem is conceived as a clock that one sets going. This idea encourages the poet to construct automated and flawless machines. Such poems have thousands of intricately moving parts, dozens of iambic belts and pulleys, precision trippers that rhyme at the right moment, lights flashing alternately red and green, steam valves that whistle like birds. This is the admired poem. Richard Wilbur, for all his ability, fell a victim to this narrow conception of the poem. His earlier "Water Walker," written before this oppressive concept of the poem penetrated him, remains his most personal and freshest poem. Robert Lowell in *Lord Weary's Castle* constructed machines of such magnitude that he found it impossible to stop them. Like the automated, chain-reacting tool of the sorcerer's apprentice, the poems will not obey. The references to Mary or Jesus that end several of them are last-minute expedients, artistically dishonest and resembling a pile of cloths thrown into a machine to stop it.

The great poets of this century have written their poems in exactly the opposite way. In the poems of Neruda, Vallejo, Jiménez, Machado, and Rilke, the poem is an extension of the substance of the man, no different from his skin or his hands. The substance of the man who wrote the poem reaches far out into the darkness and the poem is his whole body, seeing with his ears and his fingers and his hair.

Here is a poem of Machado's, written before the death of his wife; here the "I" *is* the poet.

*From the doorsill of a dream they called my
   name . . .*
It was the good voice, the voice I loved so much.

—Listen. Will you go with me to visit the soul?
A soft stroke reached up to my heart.

*—With you always . . . And in my dream I
   walked*
Down a long and solitary corridor,
Aware of the touching of the pure robe,
*And the soft beating of blood in the hand that loved
   me.*

Next, the poetry we have had in this country is a poetry without even a trace of revolutionary feeling—in either language or politics.

It is startling to realize that in the last twenty years there have been almost no poems touching on political subjects, although such concerns have been present daily. The *Kenyon Review*, under Ransom, and the *Southern Review*, under Tate, have been effective forces here. The guiding impulse in both Ransom's and Tate's minds is fear of revolution. As Southerners they act to exaggerate the fear felt by even Northerners. This kind of Southerner thinks of himself as a disinherited aristocrat. Their holding position in poetry has more resemblance to the attitude of Governor Ross Barnett of Mississippi than most people would be willing to admit. Laforgue says, "The only remedy is to break everything." Ransom says, in effect, that the only remedy is to keep everything. This is why there is so much talk of Donne and New Criticism in the *Kenyon Review*—such concerns tend to damp down any tendencies toward revolution.

Ransom remarked that he never published poems by Dylan Thomas because Thomas didn't know how to behave in a drawing room. Neruda and Brecht were not welcome in the *Kenyon Review* either.

If revolutionary thought is put down, revolution in language also dies. The absence of any interest in fresh language in literary magazines shows up in the thirties and forties. Compared with that of Hart Crane or Cummings, the language of Nemerov or Ciardi or Jarrell is inexpressibly dull. Jarrell, for example, opens a poem:

> One looks from the train
> Almost as one looked as a child. In the sunlight
> What I see still seems to me plain.

There is almost no contrast inside the line. A poet who has higher standards in language can put together inside a line words that have different natures—like strange animals together in a wood. Mallarmé uses this kind of contrast as a foundation for his poems. Awareness of the different kinds of fur that words have is instantly apparent in Lorca's poems:

> One day
> The horses will live in the saloons
> And the outraged ants
> Will throw themselves on the yellow skies that
>   have taken refuge in the eyes of cows.

Compare this with a typical stanza of ours:

> Youth comes to jingle nickels and crack wise;
> The baseball scores are his, the magazines

Devoted to lust, the jazz, the Coca-Cola,
The lending library of love's latest.
— Karl Shapiro, "The Drug Store"

In Shapiro's stanza the words are all one color: gray.

The poetry of the thirties and forties moves backward. Art Buchwald once described the scene he imagined could take place as a Fly Now–Pay Later plan collides with a failure to make a payment on time. A man from the travel agency comes to your house with a curious electric machine. You sit down in it, the current is turned on, and the machine removes all your memories of Europe. In the poetry of the thirties and forties we are supposed to forget that there were even any ideas of a different language for poetry—forget that the German expressionist poets ever lived, forget the experiments in language represented by French poets and later by Alberti and Lorca. Poetry is forgotten, if by poetry we mean exploration into the unknown, and not entertainment; an intellectual adventure of the greatest importance, not an attempt to teach manners, an attempt to face the deep inwardness of the twentieth century, not attempts to preserve the virtues of moderation. The forties generation succeeds in forgetting both the revolution in language and any revolutionary feeling toward society.

Our postwar poets defend the status quo. Nemerov, Ransom, and Ciardi, for instance, by their examples, urge poets not to make too much trouble in the universities. Ransom urges us to have a "civilized attitude." Most of these men are merely accepting the ideas of T. S. Eliot, who supports the Establishment. Hölderlin wrote a short poem on this subject, which has great common sense.

> *Deep down I despise the herd of leaders and ministers,*
> *But I despise even more the genius who takes their side.*

The poetry we have now is a poetry without the image. The only movement in American poetry that concentrates on the image was imagism, in 1911–1913. But "imagism" was largely "picturism." An image and a picture differ in that the image, being the natural speech of the imagination, cannot be drawn from or inserted back into the real world. It is an animal native to the imagination. Like Bonnefoy's "interior sea lighted by turning eagles," it cannot be seen in real life. A picture, on the other hand, is drawn from the objective "real" world. "Petals on a wet black bough" can actually be seen.

We have merely to glance at a typical American stanza of the last years to see that the image is destroyed before birth by pressure of the direct statement or the picture. John Ciardi writes,

> *Now mist takes the hemlocks and nothing*
> *stirs. This is a gray-green and a*
> *glassy thing and nothing stirs. A plane*
> *to or from Newark burrs down idling on*
> *its flaps or grinds full-rich up its*
> *airy grade, and I hear it.*

But if there is no image how is the unconscious going to make its way into the poem? Let us consider the typical "formal poem." Suppose there is no image: then such a statement in a poem as "I must perfect my will" is composed by the conscious mind, rhymes searched for and found by the conscious mind. The efficient work-aday conscious mind creates the entire poem. The important thing about an image, on the other hand, is that it is made by both the conscious and the unconscious mind. This is true of Yeats's image of the beast of the "Second Coming" and of Lorca's "the glasses of the dawn are broken."

Finally, then, our poetry has been a poetry essentially without the unconscious.

This is not surprising. Two of our strongest traditions have been puritanism (our so-called religious tradition) and business (our secular tradition). The mind of the puritan shows fear of the unconscious—a belief that only ugly and horrible images and ideas come from it. All animal life and sexual life are met with fear and disdain. These are the impulses behind the poetry of Eliot and Pound and that of the neoclassic school as well. The impulses do not describe the poetry of Hart Crane and Theodore Roethke, exceptions of almost all the points I have been making.

Max Weber showed that the apparent asceticism of the puritan had a secret purpose: to adapt the man to an efficient life in business. Working in business "ascetically" fifteen hours a day is the mark of a man who has resisted Satan; success in outward things becomes a proof of religious virtue. The drive toward outward things in the 1917 generation and in recent poets is essentially obedience to business traditions.

These two strains—puritan fear of the unconscious and the business drive toward dealing in outer things—meet in our poetry to push out the unconscious. The

1917 poets tried to adapt poetry to business and science. They looked for "formulas." They tried to deal efficiently with natural objects. They studied to develop "technical skill"—like engineers.

Then, brandishing their technical skill, the poets of the thirties and forties evict the unconscious. And poetry sinks—plunges, sometimes—into the outer world. Titles of books indicate this in an interesting way. Richard Wilbur's third book is called *Things of This World*. Shapiro titled his first book *Person, Place, and Thing*, and his new one *The Bourgeois Poet*.

IV

Ortega y Gasset in *Man and Crisis* suggests that the intellectual history of a nation hinges on the difference between generations. Members of the younger generation, when they get to be about thirty years old, find that the ideas of the older men do not seem to describe the world accurately. As the young man "meditates on the world in force" (the world of the men who in his time are mature) he finds "his problems, his doubts, are very different from those which the mature men felt in their own youth." The ideas of mature men seem false or at least no longer adequate. The men of the younger generation therefore advance their own ideas and attack the ideas of the older generation. In this debate—in which all can take part—the old ideas are examined, ideas themselves are made real, new ideas hammered out. A nation's intellectual life depends on this struggle between generations.

I have discussed briefly the generation of 1917. (Frost

and Stevens, considerably older men, belong to an earlier group.) After the 1917 generation a group of this country's poets appeared who might be called the metaphysical generation. Not only were these poets of the twenties and thirties profoundly influenced by the English metaphysical poets, but their basic attitude was detached, doctrinaire, "philosophical." Eberhart's poetry is destroyed, in most poems, by philosophical terms used with fanaticism. Poetry becomes abstract. The poet takes a step back and brings doctrines between himself and his experience. The presence of doctrines, metaphysical or political, marks both the puritan metaphysicals and the left-wing radicals—Eberhart and Tate as well as the *New Masses* poets. The interest in doctrine is all taken from the 1917 poets. Tate, for example, is a disciple of Eliot, a man nearly a decade older.

The next clearly defined generation is that of 1947— the war generation, including Karl Shapiro, Robert Lowell, John Berryman, Delmore Schwartz, Randall Jarrell, and Howard Nemerov. Their convictions about poetry are so impersonal and changeable that it would be truer to say they have no convictions at all. Ortega remarks, "Imagine a person who, when in the country, completely loses his sense of direction. He will take a few steps in one direction, then a few more in another, perhaps the exact opposite." We are reminded of Shapiro, who in his first book has a vicious attack on D. H. Lawrence; this is followed by wholehearted praise of Lawrence; his worship of New Criticism is followed by pointed disgust for it; he pursues the academic style in his own poetry, and then discards it for the Ginsberg style. Both styles are for him equally bankrupt.

The generation of 1947 might very well be called the

hysterical generation. Its response to the question of literary style or content is hysterical. In fact, hysteria itself is often a subject matter of these men's poetry, as in Berryman's *Homage to Mistress Bradstreet*. The history of Lowell's style shows the same pattern as Shapiro's. Accepting Tate's ideas, Lowell adopts a fanatically formal verse only to abandon it abruptly for the prose style of *Life Studies*. The sad fact is that he is not really fitted for either of these styles, and his own style remains undiscovered.

The progress of the generations since 1917 might then be described as the progress from the objectivist generation to the metaphysical generation to the hysterical—three clearly marked psychic steps. They are not steps toward irrationality but toward dullness and lack of conviction. They are states that succeed one another in a process of disintegration of personality. After the initial step away from inwardness, and toward the world of things, this country's poets increasingly lose touch with their own inward reality and become less and less sure of themselves. They no longer stand firmly inside their own convictions.

The outstanding characteristic of the generation of 1947 is its reluctance to criticize ideas handed to them. That new generation did not create an idea of its own. Randall Jarrell's criticism is occupied with praise of Marianne Moore and others, without any serious discussions of ideas. If Richard Wilbur has any criticism of the ideas or poetry of men older than himself, he doesn't mention it. Robert Lowell reviewed Yvor Winters's collected poems for *Poetry* and reported that the reason Winters had been left out of so many anthologies was that he is "so original and radical," an "immortal poet."

In the *Hudson Review* Lowell later gave a similar blanket endorsement of William Carlos Williams. There is something intellectually shameful about his accepting the standards of both of these men, because their standards are not only different but contradictory. Such acceptance of the ideas of older men by younger men is unnatural as well as unhealthy.

What is the result of this strange lack of intellectual struggle between the generations? Ortega remarks,

> *Entire generations falsify themselves to themselves; that is to say, they wrap themselves up in artistic styles, in doctrines, in political movements which are insincere and which fill the lack of genuine convictions. When they get to be about forty years old, these generations become null and void, because at that age one can no longer live in fictions.*

V

I have been putting forward general ideas about poetry. Let us see if these ideas hold up when poems are in front of us.

Here is an entire poem by Juan Ramón Jiménez, which has an inner intensity.

> *Music—*
> *Naked woman*
> *Running mad through the pure night!*

And here are lines in which the intensity is all on the surface:

Would you perhaps consent to be
The very rack and crucifix of winter, winter's wild
Knife-edged, continuing and unreleasing,
Intent and stripping, ice-caressing wind?
(Delmore Schwartz, "Will You Perhaps")

This is the opening of a poem by Rafael Alberti, translated by Anthony Kerrigan:

By the side of the sea and a river in my early days
I wanted to be a horse.
The reed shores were made of wind and mares.
I wanted to be a horse.

And here are lines from a recent American anthology:

The old man accepts a Lucky Strike.
He was a friend of my grandfather.
We talk of the decline of the population
And of codfish and herring.
While he waits for a herring boat to come in.
(Elizabeth Bishop, "At the Fishhouses")

In the Bishop poem we can feel the outer world driving in, invading the poem. The facts of the outer world push out the imagination and occupy the poem themselves. The lines become inflexible. The poem becomes heavy and stolid, like a toad that has eaten ball bearings.

Here are lines from *Life Studies:*

Father and Mother moved to Beverly Farms
to be a two-minute walk from the station,
half an hour by train from the Boston doctors.
(Robert Lowell, "Terminal Days at Beverly Farms")

And from Jarrell:

"In a minute the doctor will find out what is
  wrong
and cure me," the patients think as they wait.
They are patient as their name, and look childishly
And religiously at the circumstances of their hope,
The nurse, the diplomas, the old magazines.
                    (Randall Jarrell, "A Utopian Journey")

In this country's poems the facts are put in because they happened, regardless of how much they lame the poem. *Life Studies* is a very important book on the development of the outward poem, because it shows that the outward poem moves inevitably toward sociology. Here is a poem by Juan Ramón Jiménez, which makes an interesting contrast with the American sociological poem:

I am not I.
              I am this one
Walking beside me whom I do not see,
Whom at times I manage to visit,
And at other times I forget.
The one who remains silent when I talk,
The one who forgives, sweet, when I hate,
The one who takes a walk when I am indoors,
The one who will remain standing when I die.

And one of ours:

whenever he left a job,
he bought a smarter car.
Father's last employer
was Scudder, Stevens, and Clark, Investment Advisors,

himself his only client.
While Mother dragged to bed alone,
read Menninger . . .

("Commander Lowell")

This is seriously reviewed as poetry, because U.S. critics demand very little from our poets. And the poets demand very little from themselves.

Apollinaire insisted on the presence of poetry, even in four lines. His poem "Flies":

> *Our flies know all the tunes*
> *Which they learned from the flies in Norway—*
> *Those giant flies that are*
> *The divinities of the snow.*

The poem devoid of any revolutionary feeling, in politics or language, has no choice but to become descriptive prose, sociological prose—or worse, light verse. Often in recent American poetry the poet adopts a genial, joshing tone, indicating that what he is saying doesn't seem to be of any importance, even to him. To point up the difference between real poetry and what passes among us for poetry, let me quote a stanza by the Peruvian poet Vallejo, followed by a stanza in the joshing tone.

> *The anger that breaks a man down into small boys,*
> *That breaks the small boy down into equal birds,*
> *And the birds, then, into tiny eggs;*
> *The anger of the poor*
> *Owns one smooth oil against two vinegars.*

And this is the opening of a poem by Howard Nemerov in *Fifteen Modern American Poets*:

> *Her laughter was infectious; so, some found,*
> *Her love. Several young men reasonably*
> *Regret inciting her to gratitude*
> *And learning of her ardent facility.*

Poetry without inwardness or revolutionary feeling has no choice but to end in a kind of fabricated grossness. Poetry on this level of imagination must become more and more coarse to achieve sensation. Poets like Karl Shapiro are convinced that if they can only make a poem gross or outrageous enough it will be a great poem. A poem, then, becomes defined as something more prosy than prose.

> *New York, killer of poets, do you remember the day*
> *you passed me through your lower intestine? The troop*
> *train paused under Grand Central. That line of women*
> *in mink coats handed us doughnuts through the*
> *   smutty*
> *windows. They were all crying. For that I forgave New*
> *York. (We smuggled a postcard off at New Haven.)*

In this Shapiro passage the senses are completely dead. In fact, there has been a steady deadening of the senses in our poetry since 1918. There were fewer odors and colors in new poems in 1958 than there were in 1918. The absence of the senses in our poems at times is astonishing.

Here is a medieval Arabic poem called "Storm":

Each flower in the dark air opens its mouth,
Feeling about for the breasts of the abundant rain.
Meanwhile armies of the black-skinned clouds, loaded
*   with water, march by*
Majestically, bristling with the golden swords of
*   lightening.*

Here are some lines by Stanley Kunitz that are typical
of our time:

> *The compass of the ego is designed*
> *To circumscribe intact a lesser mind*
> *With definition . . .*
> *("Lovers Relentlessly")*

Abstraction is merely another form of the flight from
inwardness; the objectivist takes flight into the outward
world, and the rationalist into the efficient intellect. Rationalists try to convince us that the atrophying of the
senses is a good thing, and they describe it as the development of abstract language in poetry.

In this country intellectual statement about passion is
thought to be superior to passion—or at least equal to
it. Yvor Winters urges us to be sure our rational mind
is present when we write a poem:

A poem is good in so far as it makes a defensible rational
statement about a given human experience (the experience
need not be real but must in some sense be possible) and
at the same time communicates the emotion which ought

to be motivated by that rational understanding of the experience.

("In Defense of Reason")

Passion cannot be trusted unless taken apart and put together again by the reason. The mind will tell us what we *ought* to feel. Rilke has an entirely different vision of poetry:

> *O Lord, give each person his own personal death.*
> *A dying that moves out of the same life he lived.*
> *In which he had love, and intelligence, and trouble.*

Here are Winters's lines:

> *This passion is the scholar's heritage.*
> *The imposition of a busy age.*
> *The passion to condense from book to book*
> *Unbroken wisdom in a single look.*

The program is quite mad. If all senses died, all images die, all association with the unconscious dies, all revolutionary feeling dies, then, it is believed, we are near poetry. Let me quote as a final contrast a medieval Arabic poem—a true poem—followed by some lines of Louise Bogan.

> *Never have I seen or heard of anything like this:*
> *A pearl that changes out of modesty into a red jewel.*
>
> *Her face is so white that when you look at its beauty,*
> *You see your own face under its clear water.*

and Bogan:

> *I burned my life that I might find*
> *A passion wholly of the mind,*
> *Thought divorced from eye and bone,*
> *Ecstasy come to breath alone.*

Under the influence of objectivism and abstraction, not only does our poetry become mediocre but our criticism also. When the senses die, the sense within us that delights in poetry dies also. And it is this sense of delight that tells us whether a given group of words contains genuine poetry or not. A great poet and a great critic are like the mule who can smell fresh water ten miles away. There is a sense that tells us where the water of poetry is, abroad or at home, West or East, even under the earth.

When this sense is dead, critics have to decide whether certain books are poetry by the presence of forms, or of "important statements," or of wit, or even of length. The longer a poem is the more poetry it is thought to contain. The American lines I have quoted are often very bad and I chose them partially with that in mind. Yet in each case they show the direction of the quoted poet's work as a whole. Moreover, the very fact that the poet wrote them, printed them in a book, and allowed them to stand is evidence of the atrophying of the sense of poetry. It is possible that the American lines I have quoted are bad poetry, but another possibility is that they aren't poetry at all.

A human body, just dead, is very like a living body except that it no longer contains something that was invisible anyway. In a poem, as in a human body, what is invisible makes all the difference. The presence of poetry in words is extremely mysterious. As we know from the Japanese experience of the haiku, as well as from the experience of many brief poems in the Western tradition, poetry can be present in fifteen words, or in ten words. Length or meter or rhyme have nothing to do with it. Ungaretti has a poem of four words ("m'il-lumino / d'immenso") which is unquestionably a poem.

> Everyone stands alone on the midpoint of the earth
> pierced by a ray of sunlight;
> and suddenly it's evening.

This poem of Quasimodo's manages to slip suddenly inward.

A poem is something that penetrates for an instant into the unconscious. If it can penetrate in this way, freshly, several times, then it is a poem of several lines. But if it does not do this it is not a poem at all—no matter how long it is.

The outward poem is like a pine tree made half of tin and half of wood. The poem of things conceives itself to be describing the world correctly because there are pieces of the world in it. This poetry cannot sustain the poet or itself because the imagination has no privacy in which to grow. In the last thirty years in America the intelligence of the poet runs back and forth hurriedly between the world inside his head and the world outside. The imagination meanwhile is thinking in its chamber. The intelligence knocks at the door, demanding some imagination to put between a flat statement and a piece of glass, and rushes out with the gift. Then it hurries back to get a little more imagination to prevent two subway cars from rubbing together. The imagination is continually disturbed, torn away bit by bit, consumed like a bin or corn eaten gradually by mice.

The imagination does not want to hear these constant knockings on the door. It prefers to remain in its chamber, undisturbed, until it can create the poem all of one substance—itself. The imagination out of its own resources creates a poem as strong as the world that it faces. Rilke speaks of *"die Befreiung der dichterischen Figur,"* which may be translated as "the liberation of the poetic image," "the releasing of the image from jail." The poet is thinking of a poem in which the image is released from imprisonment among objects. The domination of the imagination is established over the entire poem. When this happens the poem enters the unconscious naturally.

Our poetry took a wrong turning years ago. Some centuries have a profound spiritual movement: poetry, when vigorous, always is a part of it. We know ours is a century of technical obsession, of business mentality, of human effort dissipated among objects, of expansion, of a destructive motion outward. Yet there is also a movement in the opposite direction that is even more powerful. The best thought in this century moves inward. This movement has been sustained by Freud, by great poetry of Europe and South America, by painting, by the most intelligent men. This is the important movement. The weakness of our poetry is that it does not share in this movement.

Most of our poetry so far has nothing to give us because, like its audience, it drifts aimlessly in the world. A country's poetry can drift outward, like the lives of most of its people, or it can plunge inward, trying for great intensity. Inward poetry deepens all life around it. Other poets have given their countries this gift. If we fail in this, of what use is our life? As Lorca says, life is not a dream.

1963

Voyages
of the
Body and Soul

An anthology of French poetry could be put together called "the Voyage into the Imagination." When Mallarmé says, "The body is sad, alas, and I have read the books," he means that he is about to start on a great voyage. The French poets in the early nineteenth century start off on a voyage into the sea of imagination. It is this voyage Mallarmé refers to when he says,

But hear, my soul, the songs of those who sail the sea.

And Baudelaire, when he says,

The perfume from the green tamarind trees
Circles in the air, and loads my nostrils,
And mingles in my soul with the songs of the men of
the sea.

It is this sea voyage that sets off French poetry so sharply from most of the poetry we study in school.

Most of the poetry written since the rationalists and pragmatists took over language resembles a trip on land. On land one is surrounded on all sides by recognizable objects. But when one enters the sea, the back is turned to recognizable objects and the face to something else.

When French poets embarked on this voyage they received an insight into soul, into the waters of grief, the energies below and beyond the established bounds. Rimbaud is not admirable because he took dope or because he shouted "*Merde!*" during certain poetry readings—although that was admirable too—but because he grasped the deep interior life flowing beneath the reason.

Here is a poem by de Nerval, called "Golden Lines."

"Astonishing! Everything is intelligent!"

—Pythagoras

Free thinker! Do you think you are the only thinker
On this earth in which life blazes inside all things?
Your liberty does what it wishes with the powers it
     controls,
But when you gather to plan, the universe is not there.

Look carefully in an animal at a spirit alive;
Every flower is a soul opening out into nature;
A mystery touching love is asleep inside metal;
"Everything is intelligent!" And everything moves
     you.

In that blind wall, look out for the eyes that pierce you;
The substance of creation cannot be separated from a
     word . . .
Do not force it to labor in some low phrase!

Often a Holy Thing is living hidden in a dark creature;
And like an eye which is born covered by its lids,
A pure spirit is growing strong under the bark of
  stones!

That is my own translation, clear but utterly inadequate to the resonance of the original. Here is Baudelaire's famous poem on resonances, which I have translated under the title "Intimate Associations."

Nature is a holy place, where the living pillars
Let slip at times some strangely garbled words;
Man walks there through forests of physical things that
  are also spiritual things,
They watch him with affectionate looks.

As the echoes of great bells coming from far away
Become entangled in a deep and profound association,
A merging as huge as night, or as huge as clear light,
Odors and colors and sounds all mean—each other.

Perfumes exist that are as cool as the flesh of infants,
Fragile as oboes, green as open fields,
And others exist also, corrupt, dense, and triumphant,

Having the associations of infinite things,
Such as musk and amber, myrrh and incense,
That describe the voyages of the body and soul.

No matter how much we admire the worldly, satiric and prudent poetry written in the industrial democracies, we can feel that some kind of magnificence or transcendence is missing in much of it—in fact, infinity is missing. We have poems about our grandfathers and grandmothers arriving on ships, and our fathers making money, but few about Gnostic ideas, mythological thought, neoplatonic histories, "anima mundi."

If we go back a generation or two, we notice that Pound and Marianne Moore were not interested in the "voyage" or in the "Holy Thing," or in the "merging as huge as clear light," or in the kindness and gentleness that often mark those who start off on such a voyage. Our inheritance has been the anger of early Eliot, the isolation of Berryman and Plath.

The latent intelligence holds in itself not only horrifying visions, which Freud reported with such satisfaction, but also affection, and discipline, and beyond that the "eternal love" one senses in *Tristan and Isolde*. It is not only in tradition and history that we find dedication to value, loyalty to beauty and human warmth. Eliot and Pound demand established tradition, and imply that ugly and horrible things, and those only, come out of their unconscious; and Eliot declares that Blake was foolish to trust his private visions. Commenting recently on a collection of contemporary German poetry, Anthony Hecht, a poet of my own age who follows Eliot's lead, writes,

The fantastic and hideous images from the unconscious certainly have their place in poetry, and they are no doubt universally available. The dear old gentleman who faithfully brings crumbs to the pigeons in winter may have nightmares as foul as the next man, and Bosch knew very well how monstrous and vivid these presences might be to a saint in the desert. They are demons, our own secret evil longings, and they are very real. But these images exist outside of time, eternally, everywhere, and in their submerged and terrible domain we are pretty much alike. It is history that makes us, or lets us be, what we are uniquely, and gives to our lives their singular stamps and profiles.

We gather from this that our duty as civilized people is to avoid "fantastic and hideous images," and depend on history to steady us, and avoid too much free thinking. This attitude was stated by Eliot forcefully in *After Strange Gods*, where he associated free thinking with the Jews. The fear of anything outside "history" is present in a subterranean way in Pound's work, and it has a part in his anti-Semitism also.

We know that the latent intelligence, or the biological reservoir of experiences, touches our instinctive life, and through that the life of all animals. The conservative doctrine suggests the world of instincts and animals is basically evil. How far this is from the "Golden Lines" of de Nerval! The attitudes could hardly be more opposed.

Eliot's and Pound's prose about French poetry gives a false impression of it. Most persons take their view of Laforgue principally from Eliot—with notions of futility, cosmic irony, self-deprecation, alienation, and so on. But Laforgue's work has great love as well, love of women and of nature; there is great gusto in his view of his own maleness. This joyfulness, kindness, and humanness is visible even in the poems when translated. It is not essentially different from the mood of trust in the animal world that moves through de Nerval's poem "Golden Lines" or Baudelaire's poem on correspondences.

The "mysterious poets"—de Nerval, Baudelaire, Rimbaud, and Mallarmé—form a continual flow through the entire nineteenth century, moving on the life that moves beneath the historical world. Corbiere is not a part of this, and it is Corbiere's work that Eliot's work most resembles. His self-hatreds and self-mockeries are genuinely meant.

Fear of instinctual life belongs to the puritan reservoir. It entered, or reentered, American literature in the twenties at an unexpected angle, carried by Eliot and Pound, who represented it as part of European avant-garde literature. The fear has multiplied in poets after Eliot and Pound. Fear of instinctual life dominates the world of Yvor Winters, and through Winters and Tate was communicated to Robert Lowell. His translations of French poetry are noticeable, over and beyond their remarkable verbal energy, for the willful distortion of French images in the direction of violence and self-dislike.

I intend this essay as a contribution toward debate of the question, Why hasn't American poetry brought the remarkable "voyage" or "descent" poetry of the French into our bloodstream? Some of the cold and fruitless occultism of the French appears in James Merrill's poetry, and John Ashbery's work carries their dadaistic fragmentation and barren algebra of image. But neither of those nourishments are the true food. *Sulphur* defends Spanish-language food at times. But most poets of the eighties go around and around in a circle like an old horse in a mill; they lack "ambition" as Donald Hall said in his brilliant piece "Poetry and Ambition." The poetry takes small steps and walks slowly. Some workshop poets have apparently eaten positivist language cakes cooked by Locke and Dewey, and they end up blind and crippled. Where do we go to find poetry that flies?

1961

Looking
for Dragon Smoke

I

In ancient times, in the "time of inspiration," the poet flew from one world to another, "riding on dragons," as the Chinese said. Isaiah rode on those dragons, so did Li Po and Pindar. They dragged behind them long tails of dragon smoke. Some of the dragon smoke still boils out of *Beowulf:* The *Beowulf* poet holds tight to Danish soil, or leaps after Grendel into the sea.

This dragon smoke means that a leap has taken place in the poem. In many ancient works of art we notice a long floating leap at the center of the work. That leap can be described as a leap from the conscious to the latent intelligence and back again, a leap from the known part of the mind to the unknown part and back to the known. In the epic of Gilgamesh, which takes place in a settled society, psychic forces create Enkidu, "the hairy man," as a companion for Gilgamesh, who is becoming too successful. The reader has to leap back and forth between the golden man, "Gilgamesh," and the "hairy man." In the *Odyssey* the travelers visit a Great Mother island, dominated by the Circe-Mother and get turned into pigs. They make the leap in an instant. In all art derived from Great Mother mysteries, the leap to the unknown part of the mind lies in the very center of the world. The strength of "classic art" has much more to do with this leap than with the order that the poets developed to contain, and partially, to disguise it.

In terms of language, leaping is the ability to associate fast. In a great poem, the considerable distance between the associations, that is, the distance the spark has to leap, gives the lines their bottomless feeling, their space, and the speed (of the association) increases the excitement of the poetry.

As Christian civilization took hold, and the power of the spiritual patriarchies deepened, this leap occurred less and less often in Western literature. Obviously, the ethical ideas of Christianity inhibit it. At the start most Church fathers were against the leap as too pagan. Ethics usually support campaigns against the "animal instincts." Christian thought, especially Paul's thought, builds a firm distinction between spiritual energy and animal energy, a distinction so sharp it became symbolized by black and white. White became associated with the conscious and black with the unconscious or the latent intelligence. Ethical Christianity taught its poets—we are among them—to leap *away* from the unconscious, not *toward* it.

II

Sometime in the thirteenth century, poetry in England began to show a distinct decline in the ability to associate powerfully. There are individual exceptions, but the circle of worlds pulled into the poem by association dwindles after Chaucer and Langland; their work is already a decline from the *Beowulf* poet. By the eighteenth century, freedom of association had become drastically curtailed. The word "sylvan" by some psychic coupling leads directly to "nymph," to "lawns," to "dancing," so does "reason" to "music," "spheres," "heavenly order," and so on. They are all stops on the psychic railroad. There are very few images of the Snake, or the Dragon, or the Great Mother, and if mention is made, the Great Mother leads to no other images, but rather to words suggesting paralysis or death. As Pope warned his readers: "The proper study of mankind is man."

The loss of associative freedom shows itself in form as well as in content. The poet's thought plods through the poem, line after line, like a man being escorted through a prison. The rigid "form" resembles a corridor, interrupted by opening and closing doors. The rhymed lines open at just the right moment and closes again behind the visitors.

In the eighteenth century many educated people in Europe were no longer interested in imagination. They were trying to develop the "masculine" mental powers they associated with Socrates and his fellow Athenians—a demythologized intelligence, that moves in a straight line made of tiny bright links and is thereby dominated by linked facts rather than by "irrational" feelings. The Europeans succeeded in developing the practical intellect, and it was to prove useful. Industry needed it to guide a locomotive through a huge freight yard; space engineers needed it later to guide a spaceship back from the moon through the "reentry corridor."

III

Nevertheless, this routing of psychic energy away from "darkness" and the "irrational," first done in obedience to Christian ethics, and later in obedience to industrial needs, had a crippling effect on the psychic life. The process amounted to an inhibiting of psychic flight, and as Blake saw, once the European child had finished ten years of school, he was incapable of flight. He lived the rest of his life with "single vision and Newton's sleep."

The Western mind after Descartes accepted the symbolism of white and black and far from trying to unite both in a circle, as the Chinese did, tried to create an "apartheid." In the process words sometimes took on strange meanings. If a European avoided the animal instincts and consistently leapt away from the latent intelligence, he or she was said to be living in a state of "innocence." Children were thought to be "innocent." Eighteenth-century translators like Pope and Dryden forced Greek and Roman literature to be their allies in their leap away from animality, and they translated Homer as if he too were "innocent." To Christian Europeans, impulses open to the sexual instincts or animal instincts indicated a fallen state, a state of "experience."

Blake thought the nomenclature mad, the precise opposite of the truth, and he wrote *The Songs of Innocence and Experience* to say so. Blake, discussing "experience," declared that to be afraid of a leap into the unconscious is actually to be in a state of "experience." (We are all experienced in that fear.) The state of "experience" is characterized by blocked love-energy, boredom, envy, and joylessness. Another characteristic is the pedestrian movement of the mind; possibly constant fear makes the mind move slowly. Blake could see that after 1,800 years of no leaping, joy was disappearing, poetry was dying, "the languid strings do scarcely move! The sound is forced, the notes are few." A nurse in the state of "experience," obsessed with a fear of animal blackness (a fear that increased after the whites took Africa), and some sort of abuse in her childhood, calls the children in from play as soon as the light falls:

> When the voices of children are heard on the green
> And whisp'rings are in the dale,
> The days of my youth rise fresh in my mind,
> My face turns green and pale.
>
> Then come home, my children, the sun is gone
>   down
> And the dews of night arise;
> Your spring and your day are wasted in play
> And your winter and night in disguise.

The nurse in *The Songs of Innocence* also calls the children in. But she has conquered her fear and when the children say,

> "No, no, let us play, for it is yet day
> And we cannot go to sleep:
> Besides in the sky the little birds fly
> And the hills are all cover'd with sheep."

She replies (the children's arguments are quite convincing),

> "Well, well, go and play till the light fades away
> And then go home to bed."

The little ones leaped and shouted and laugh'd
And all the hills echoed.

She enjoys their shouts. The children leap about on the grass playing, and the hills respond.

We often feel elation when reading Homer, Neruda, Dickinson, Vallejo, and Blake because the poet is following some arc of association that corresponds to the inner life of the objects he or she speaks of, for example, the association between the lids of eyes and the bark of stones. The associative paths are not private to the poet, but are somehow inherent in the universe.

IV

An ancient work of art such as the *Odyssey* has at its center a long floating leap, around which the poem's images gather themselves like steel shavings around a magnet. Some recent works of art have many shorter leaps rather than one long one. The poet who is "leaping" makes a jump from an object soaked in conscious psychic substance to an object soaked in latent or instinctive psychic substance. One real joy of poetry—not the only one—is to experience this leaping inside a poem.

Novalis, Goethe, and Hölderlin, writing around 1800 in Germany, participated in the associative freedom I have been describing; and their thought in a parallel way carried certain pagan and heretical elements, precisely as Blake's thought did at that time in England. A century later Freud pointed out that the dream still retained the fantastic freedom of association known to most educated Europeans only from pre-Christian poetry and art. We notice that dream interpretation has never been a favorite occupation of the fundamentalists.

In psychology of the last eighty years the effort to recover the dream's freedom of association and its metaphors has been partly successful. Some of the psychic ability to go from the known to the unknown part of the psyche and back has been restored. So too the "leaping" poets: Rilke and Bobrowski, Lorca, and Vallejo, Rene Char, Yves Bonnefoy, and Paul Celan.

Yeats, riding on the dragonish associations of Irish mythology, wrote genuinely great poetry. If we, in the United States, cannot learn dragon smoke from Yeats, or from the French descenders, or from the Spanish leapers, from whom will we learn it? I think much is at stake in this question.

Let's set down some of the enemies that leaping has in this country. American fundamentalism is against the journey to dark places; capitalism is against the descent to soul; realism is against the leap to spirit; populism and social thought are against the solitary wildness; careerism in poetry doesn't allow enough time for descent; group thought will not support individual ventures; the reluctance of recent American poets to translate makes them ignorant. We notice that contemporary American poets tend to judge their poetry by comparing it to the poetry other people of their time are writing—their reviews make this clear—rather than by comparing their work to Goethe's, or Akhmatova's, or Tsvetaeva's or Blake's. Great poetry always has something of the grandiose in it. It's as if American poets are now so distrustful of the grandiose and so afraid to be thought grandiose that they cannot even imagine great poetry.

V

Lorca wrote a beautiful and great essay called "Theory and Function of the Duende," available in English in the Penguin edition of Lorca. "Duende" is the sense of the presence of death, and Lorca says,

Very often intellect is poetry's enemy because it is too much given to imitation, because it lifts the poet to a throne of sharp edges and makes him oblivious of the fact that he may suddenly be devoured by ants, or a great arsenic lobster may fall on his head.

Duende involves a kind of elation when death is present in the room. It is associated with "dark" sounds; and when a poet has duende inside him, he brushes past death with each step, and in that presence associates fast (Samuel Johnson remarked that there was nothing like a sentence of death in half an hour to wonderfully concentrate the mind). The gypsy flamenco dancer is associating fast when she dances, and so is Bach writing his cantatas. Lorca mentions an old gypsy dancer who, on hearing Brailowsky play Bach, cried out, "That has duende!"

The Protestant embarrassment in the presence of death turns us into muse poets or angel poets, associating timidly. Lorca says,

The duende—where is the duende? Through the empty arch comes an air of the mind that blows insistently over the heads of the dead, in search of the new landscapes and unsuspected accents; an air smelling of child's saliva,

*of pounded grass, and medusal veil announcing the con-
stant baptism of newly created things.*

The Spanish "surrealist" or "leaping" poet often enters
into his poem with a heavy body of feeling piled up
behind him as if behind a dam. Some of that water is
duende water. The poet enters the poem excited, with
the emotions alive; he is angry or ecstatic, or disgusted.
There are a lot of exclamation marks, visible or invisible.
Almost all the poems in Lorca's *Poet in New York* are
written with the poet profoundly moved, flying. Powerful feeling makes the mind move, fast, and evidently
the presence of swift motion makes the emotions still
more alive, just as chanting awakens many emotions
that the chanter was hardly aware of at the moment he
began chanting.

What is the opposite of wild association then? Tame
association? Approved association? Sluggish association? Whatever we want to call it, we know what it is—
that slow plodding association that pesters us in so
many poetry magazines, and in our own work when it
is no good, association that takes half an hour to compare a childhood accident to a crucifixion, or a leaf to
the *I Ching*. Poetry is killed for students in high school
by teachers who only understand this dull kind of association.

Lorca says,

*To help us seek the duende there are neither maps nor
discipline. All one knows is that it burns the blood like
powdered glass, that it exhausts, that it rejects all the
sweet geometry one has learned, that it breaks with all
styles . . . that it dresses the delicate body of Rimbaud in*

an acrobat's green suit: or that it puts the eyes of a dead fish on Count Lautreamont in the early morning Boulevard.

The magical quality of a poem consists in its being always possessed by the duende, so that whoever beholds it is baptized with dark water.

1967–1972

Poetry

and

the Three Brains

I

Researchers and neurologists have made in the last two decades discoveries about the brain that are astonishing. Paul MacLean's work, immense in its implications, has been discussed in numerous scientific articles and books, but the literary community has not paid much attention to it. He has identified three brain structures— ancient, relatively recent, and new. I'll sum up here a few of his thoughts on these structures or "brains."

The brain system, one can say, preserves and maintains: it discards no old structures, but conserves them, and reassigns each to its task. The oldest brain structure, which we will call the reptile brain, is still very much energized, in use, and intact. It is a horseshoe shaped organ located in the base of the skull. The job of the reptile brain appears to be the physical survival of the organism in which it finds itself. Should danger or enemies come near, an alarm system comes into play, and the reptile brain takes over from the other brains—it takes what we might call "executive power." In great danger it might hold that power exclusively. It's been noticed, for example, that when mountain climbers are in danger of falling, the brain mood changes—the eyesight intensifies, and the feet "miraculously" take the right steps. Once down, the climber realizes he has been "blanked out." This probably means that the reptile brain's need for energy was so great that it withdrew energy even from the memory systems of the mammal and new brains. The presence of fear produces a higher energy input to the reptile brain. The increasing fear in this century means that more and more energy, as a result, is going to the reptile brain: that is the same thing, in effect, as saying that the military budgets in all nations are increasing.

MacLean himself speculated, in a paper written recently for a philosophical conference, that the persistent trait of paranoia in human beings is due to the inability to shut off the energy source to the reptile brain. In a settled society, if there are no true enemies, the reptile brain will imagine enemies in order to preserve and use its share of the incoming energy. John Foster Dulles represented the reptile brain in the fifties.

When the change to mammal life occurred, a second brain was simply folded around the reptile node. This limbic node which I will call here the mammal brain, fills most of the skull. The mammal brain has quite different functions. When we come to the mammal brain we find for the first time a sense of community: men and women's love for each other, friendship, passion, love of children, of the neighbor, the idea of brotherhood, care for the community or for the country. "There is no greater love than that of a man who will lay down his life for a friend." Evidently in the mammal brain there are two nodes of energy: sexual love and ferocity. (The reptile brain has no ferocity: it simply fights coldly for survival.) Women have strong mammal brains and probably a correspondingly smaller energy channel to the reptile brain. But they are fierce. The sixties supported the mammal brain. "Make love, not war" means "move from the reptile brain to the mammal brain." Rock music is mammal music for the most part; long hair is mammal hair.

The Viking warrior who went "berserk" in battle may have experienced the temporary capture of himself by the mammal brain. Eye witnesses reported that the face of the "berserk" appeared to change, and his strength increased fantastically—when he "woke up," he sometimes found he had killed twenty or thirty men. The facial expression is probably a union of the concerns of all three brains, so if one brain takes over, it is natural that the shape of the face would change.

What does the third brain, the "new brain" do? In late mammal times, the body evidently added a third brain. Brain researchers are not sure why—perhaps the addition is connected to the invention of tools and the energy explosion that followed that. In any case, this third brain, which I shall call here the new brain, takes the form of an outer eighth inch of brain tissue laid over the surface of the mammal brain. It is known medically as the neocortex. Brain tissue of the neocortex is incredibly complicated, more so than the other brains, having millions of neurons per square inch. Curiously, the third brain seems to have been created for problems more complicated than those it is now being used for. Some neurologists speculate that an intelligent man today uses 1/100 of its power. Einstein may have been using 1/50 of it.

The only good speculations I have seen on the new brain, and what it is like, are in Charles Fair's book, *The Dying Self*. Fair suggests that what Freud meant by the "Id" was the reptile and mammal brain, and what the ancient Indian philosophers meant by the "self" was the new brain. His book is fascinating. He thinks that the new brain can grow and that its food is wild spiritual ideas. Christ said, "If a seed goes into the ground and dies, then it will grow." The reptile and mammal brains don't understand that sentence at all, both being naturalists, but the new brain understands it, and feels the excitement of it. The Greek mystery religions and the Essene cult that Christ was a member of were clear attempts to feed the new brain. The "mysteries" were the religion of the new brain. In Europe the new brain reached its highest energy point about 1500, after knowing the ecstatic spiritual ideas of the Near East for seven hundred years. The "secularization" since then means that the other two brains have increased their power. Nevertheless, a people may still live if they wish to more in their new brain than their neighbors do. Many of the parables of Christ and the remarks of Buddha evidently involve instructions on how to transfer energy from the reptile brain to the mammal brain, and then to the new brain. A "saint" is someone who has managed to move away from the reptile and the mammal brains and is living primarily in the new brain. As the reptile brainpower is symbolized by cold and the mammal brain by warmth, the mark of the new brain is light. The gold light always around Buddha's head in statues is an attempt to suggest that he is living in his new brain. Some Tibetan meditators of the thirteenth century were able to read books in the dark by the light given off from their own bodies.

II

If there is no central organization to the brain, it is clear that the three brains must be competing for all available energy at any moment. The brains are like legislative committees—competing for government funds. A separate decision on apportionment is made in each head, although the whole tone of the society has weight on that decision. Whichever brain receives the most energy, that brain will determine the tone of that personality, regardless of his intelligence or "reasoning power." The United States, given the amount of fear it generates every day in its own citizens as well as in the citizens of other nations, is a vast machine for throwing people into the reptile brain. The ecology workers, poets, singers, meditators, rock musicians, and many people in the younger generation in general are trying desperately to reverse the contemporary energy flow in the brain. Military appropriations cannot be reduced until the flow of energy in the brain, which has been moving for four or five centuries from the new brain to the reptile brain, is reversed. The reptile and the new brains are now trying to make themselves visible. The reptile has embodied itself in the outer world in the form of a tank that even moves like a reptile. Perhaps the computer is the new brain desperately throwing itself out into the world of objects so that we'll *see* it; the new brain's spirituality could not be projected, but at least its speed is apparent in the computer. The danger, of course, with the computer is that it may fall into the power of the reptile brain. Nixon is a dangerous type— a mixture of reptile and new brain, with almost no mammal brain at all. Bush is reptilian also, with a weaker new brain.

III

We do not spend the whole day "inside" one brain, but we flip perhaps a thousand times a day from one brain to the other. Moreover, we have been doing this flipping so long—since we were in the womb—that we no longer recognize the flips when they occur. If there is no central organization to the brain, and evidently there is not, it means that there is no "I." If your name is John there is no "John" inside you—there is no "I" at all. Oddly, that is the fundamental idea that Buddha had thirteen hundred years ago. "I have news for you," he said, "there is no 'I' inside there. Therefore trying to find it is useless." The West misunderstands "meditation" or sitting because, being obsessed with unity and "identity," it assumes that the purpose of meditation is to achieve unity. On the contrary, the major value of sitting, particularly at the start, is to let the sitter experience the real chaos of the brain. Thoughts shoot in from all three brains in turn, and the sitter does not talk about, but *experiences*, the lack of an "I." The lack of an "I" is a central truth of Buddhism (Taoism expresses it by talking of the presence of a "flow"). Christianity somehow never arrived at this idea. At any rate, it never developed practical methods, like sitting, to allow each person to experience the truth himself. Institutional Christianity is in trouble because it depends on a pre-Buddhist model of the brain.

IV

Evidently spiritual growth for human beings depends on the ability to transfer energy. Energy that goes normally to the reptile brain can be transferred to the mammal brain, some of it at least; energy intended for the mammal brain can be transferred to the new brain.

The reptile brain thinks constantly of survival, of food, of security. When Christ says, "Consider the lilies, how they grow; they neither toil nor spin, and yet Solomon in all his glory was never dressed like one of these," he is urging his students not to care so much for themselves. If the student wills "not caring," and that "not caring" persists, the "not caring" will eventually cause some transfer of energy away from the reptile brain. Voluntary poverty worked for St. Francis, and he had so little reptile brain paranoia that the birds came down to sit on his shoulders.

If energy has been diverted from the reptile brain, the student, if he is lucky, can then transfer some of it to the mammal, and then to the new brain. Christ once advised his students, "If someone slaps you on the left cheek, point to the right cheek." The mammal brain loves to flare up and to strike back instantly. If you consistently refuse to allow the ferocity of the mammal brain to go forward into action, it will become discouraged, and some of its energy will be available for transfer. Because the mammal brain commits a lot of its energy to sexual love, some men and women at this point in the "road" become ascetic and celibate. They do so precisely to increase the speed of energy transfer. Saints such as Anna of Foligno, experienced this same turn in the road, which usually involves an abrupt abandonment of husband and children. Christ remarks in *The Gospel of Thomas* that some men are born eunuchs, and some men make themselves eunuchs to get to the Kingdom of the Spirit. However if a man is in the reptile brain at the time he begins his asceticism, then the result is a psychic disaster, as it has been for so many Catholic priests and monks.

The leap from the reptile to the new brain cannot be made directly; the student must go through the mammal brain. St. Theresa's spiritual prose shows much sexual imagery, perhaps because the mammal brain contributed its energy to the spiritual brain.

"Meditation" is a practical method for transferring energy from the reptile to the mammal brain, and then from the mammal to the new brain. It is slow, but a "wide" road, a road many can take, and many religious disciplines have adopted it. The Orientals do not call it meditation, but "sitting." If the body sits in a room for an hour, quietly, doing nothing, the reptile brain becomes increasingly restless. It wants battle, danger. In Oriental meditation the body is sitting in the fetal position, and this further infuriates the reptile brain, because it is basically a mammalian position.

Of course, if the sitter continues to sit, the mammal brain quickly becomes restless too. It wants excitement, confrontations, insults, sexual joy. It now starts to feed in spectacular erotic imagery, of the sort that St. Anthony's sittings were famous for. Yet if the sitter persists in doing nothing, eventually energy has nowhere to go but to the new brain.

Because Christianity has no "sitting," fewer men and women in Western culture than in Oriental civilizations have been able to experience the ecstasy of the new brain. Thoreau managed to transfer a great deal of energy to the new brain without meditation, merely with the help of solitude. Solitude evidently helps the new brain. Thoreau, of course, willed his solitude and he was not in a reptile city, but in mammal or "mother" nature. Once more the truth holds that the road to the new brain passes through the mammal brain, through "the forest." This truth is embodied in ancient literature by the tradition of spiritual disciples meditating first in the forest and only after that in the desert. For the final part of the road, the desert is useful, because it contains almost no mammal images. Even in the desert, however, the saints preferred to live in caves—perhaps to remind the reptile brain of the path taken.

V

It's possible that just as a politician could be dominated by one or two of the brains, so too a poet. The reptile brain doesn't seem to produce many great poets that support it, but Robinson Jeffers will have to do. His mammal brain is really marvelous, but he often declared that he preferred hawks, sharks, and killer whales to people. He loved the beaks tearing at soft flesh.

*Eagle and hawk with their great claws and hooked
     heads
Tear life to pieces . . .*

The mammal brain, without much reptile, gives the
warmth and grief to Chaucer and Villon, to Anna Akhmatova, Emily Dickinson, Hart Crane, Thomas Hardy,
and Keats. We can feel the light of the new brain pouring
off St. John of the Cross, Kabir, Mirabai, St. Francis, St.
Theresa, Rub'ia, Rumi, Angelius Silesius, Bashō, and
Bach.

Some poets write of the progress from reptile to mammal to new brain, or the regression backward. Blake
invented a being called Urizen whose coldness, rigidity,
and reptilian blindness to feeling is a superb description
of the human being who is "fallen," that is regressed.
The reptile brain may be the "invisible worm":

> *The invisible worm*
> *That flies in the night,*
> *In the howling storm,*
> *Has found out thy bed*
> *Of crimson joy,*
> *And his dark secret love*
> *Does thy life destroy.*

Lorca often describes the forward motion, the cockroach
who wants to be a butterfly.

We notice that MacLean's triune structure of the brain
throws light particularly on the sort of poetry we have
called associative or leaping. Lorca in the following passage gives the mood of the mammal brain in the first

line, and then leaps to a picture taken from the memory banks of the reptile brain.

> *The creatures of the moon sniff and prowl about*
> *their cabins.*
> *The living iguanas will come to bite the men who do*
> *not dream,*

Then in the third and fourth lines he puts human warmth right next to the "alligator"

> *and the man who rushes out with his spirit broken will*
> *meet on the street corner*
> *the unbelievable alligator quiet beneath the tender*
> *protest of the stars . . .*

This is very impressive. The associative paths, so ignored in North American poetry, allow us to leap from one part of the brain to another and lay out their contraries. Moreover it's possible that what we call "mythology" deals precisely with these abrupt juxtapositions.

Great poetry activates energy from the ancient, recent, and new brain structures by using images appropriate to that particular memory system. Then, using what Joseph Campbell called "mythological thinking," it moves the energy along the spectrum—either up or down. Such poetry can awaken the "lost music," walk on the sea, cross the river from instinct to spirit. It can fly across interior spaces as dragons fly over water and touch the dark wheels of intelligence and set them moving, so that poetry does not settle for being a scholarly comment on life, but becomes, as in Shakespeare, a form of life.

This wildness is what draws a young man or woman to poetry, and holds him or her there. I am not offering these ideas as a quick way to write great poetry. The road to leaping is a difficult road. I wrote a long poem a few years ago and was so interested in the leaping that I never figured out what the subject was.

No matter how much we know of association, or leaping, or brain systems, we still have to make our poem out of that place where some genuine grief has reached out and touched us. Perhaps we even make the poem from our slow place, our slowest place. Or, as Thomas McGrath and Etheridge Knight do, we make it out of the sorrow of the world. The Brazilian samba provides in the midst of its passion a four-beat pause where all drumming and dancing stop, and it is said that in the pause we sink down and feel the sorrow of the world.

The mention of sorrow brings us back to where we began, the old black dress of realism. This time it is the black dress of sorrow:

> *Ach, Mutter,*
> *this old black dress,*
> *I have been embroidering*
> *French flowers on it.*

1972–1989

PART TWO

The Bread of
This World: Twelve
Contemporary Poets

James Wright
and the Mysterious Woman

When I first met and got to know James Wright—we met in 1958 and became friends in 1959—the psychic placidity, part blindness, part arrogance, that had been a quality of the fifties was still very much alive. On the other hand, the obsession with T. S. Eliot was declining and the fascination with English metrical verse, which was still strong in 1950, had begun to fade. A feminine being whom I will call the Mysterious Hidden Woman began to rise from the earth around that time. I would call her appearance the major cultural event of the late fifties and early sixties. She belongs to no particular culture and rises and falls in the human psyche as she wishes. One could call her Aphrodite, or the Delicate One, or Sophia. Whatever we call her she is helpful to poetry.

She appeared strongly and sweetly in Spain in 1890 or so to 1937. Antonio Machado noticed her:

> Close to the road we sit down one day.
> Our whole life now amounts to understanding time,
>   and our sole concern

> The attitudes of despair that we adopt
> while we wait. But She will not fail to arrive.

Juan Ramón Jiménez said,

> *Music: a naked woman*
> *running mad through the pure night!*

Lorca inherited her from Machado and Jiménez and he made marvelous rooms in his poems for her. Her quality includes a lightness, an innocence, and a remembrance of the good parts of childhood. Lorca said,

> *My heart of silk*
> *is filled with lights*
> *with lost bells,*
> *with lilies and bees.*
> *I will go very far,*
> *farther than those mountains,*
> *farther than the oceans,*
> *way up near the stars,*
> *to ask Christ the Lord*
> *to give back to me*
> *the soul I had as a child,*
> *matured by fairy tales,*
> *with its hat of feathers*
> *and its wooden sword.*

Around 1960 James wrote this poem.

SPRING IMAGES

> *Two athletes*
> *Are dancing in the cathedral*
> *Of the wind.*

A butterfly lights on the branch
Of your green voice.

Small antelopes
Fall asleep in the ashes
Of the moon.

The first stanza is best. If you say it aloud, you can feel her mood. She is in the "ee"s.

Two athletes
Are dancing in the cathedral
Of the wind.

During these years James was teaching English at the University of Minnesota. He would often on the weekends take a train from Minneapolis to Montevideo, where Carol and I would meet him and take him to the farm. We would usually talk half the night, and then in the late morning take a walk out in the fields. He would work on poems in "the chicken house"—my study, which had once sheltered chickens. Then in the late afternoon we would walk again, at dusk. Here is a poem he wrote called "Beginning" after one of those walks.

The moon drops one or two feathers into the field.
The dark wheat listens.
Be still.
Now.
There they are, the moon's young, trying
Their wings.
Between trees, a slender woman lifts up the
   lovely shadow

> *Of her face, and now she steps into the air,*
>   *now she is gone*
> *Wholly, into the air.*
> *I stand alone by an elder tree, I do not*
>   *dare breathe*
> *Or move.*
> *I listen.*
> *The wheat leans back toward its own darkness,*
> *And I lean toward mine.*

We never discussed this "woman" in the terms I am using now. We were both aware however that something was changing, had changed, in our own psychic houses, as well as outside in the culture. The trees and field don't change; but it is as if we have new eyes for what is there, or rather new *ears*.

> *The moon drops one or two feathers into the field.*
> *The dark wheat listens.*

The next line is

> *Be still.*

The man or woman to whom she comes feels an inexplicable trust in the world. That trust does not extend to people; in a way one feels safe *from* people precisely because of the enclosing shield she offers, or because she carries with her an assurance that the life of the earth is good, whatever cruelty people embody.

The fragrance of the Chinese attempt to describe her presence drifted into James's poems, and that fragrance helped to heal some old wound of his. This is a poem called "American Wedding":

> She dreamed long of waters.
> Inland today, she wakens
> On scraped knees, lost
> Among locust thorns.
>
> She gropes for
> The path backward, to
> The pillows of the sea.
>
> Bruised trillium
> Of wilderness, she
> May rest on briar leaves,
> As long as the wind cares to pause.
>
> Now she is going to learn
> How it is that animals
> Can save time:
> They sleep a whole season
> Of lamentation and snow,
> Without bothering to weep.

Li Po referred to her when he said,

> If you were to ask me why I dwell among green
>   mountains,
> I should laugh silently; my soul is serene.
> The peach blossom follows the moving water;
> There is another heaven and earth beyond the world of
>   men.
>
> (translated by Robert Payne)

James wrote poems, and tried to write poems, that honored Her. Her poetry has its own delicacy and requires—or so he felt at least—its own lightly touching language, an absence of the closure given by the couplet, and a childlike syntax.

James could feel in Whitman a delicacy and vulnerability that he now valued even more than he had before, but that admiration was not at that time welcome in some academic circles. I remember that he arrived at the house one Friday night looking depressed. "What's wrong?" I said.

"Oh," he said, "I went to a party last night at Allen Tate's, with a lot of English department people. In the course of it, I made a mistake. I said something complimentary about Whitman. I should have known better."

"What happened?"

"There was a silence in the room. It was interesting that not one of the men said anything. Finally one of the department wives burst out and said, 'Just name one poem of Whitman's that is good—just one!' speaking for the offended husbands.

"I should have known better," Jim said. "What was the matter with me?"

I don't think this was paranoia; he was reporting events.

After one or two of his new poems had been published in *Poetry* or somewhere, he went to New York for a reading, followed by a literary gathering, and he told a somewhat similar story. In the middle of the party one of the poets our age came up to him and spoke of James's new poems with real venom. Jim laughed as he told the story, and said, "Listen, Robert, this is weird:

relaxation and gentleness in a poem produces in some people real fear and rage."

There are readers who want all poems to be desperate and bitter; and if they aren't, it ruins the party. Without being mythical about it, we could say that in the literary community, where the very process of studying poetry often increases one's store of irony, ambiguity, wariness, and anger, there is a kind of low-level conspiracy to keep out of view the poems of tenderness and quiet. That surely contributed to Robert Penn Warren's decision to include no Whitman poems at all in his first edition of *Understanding Poetry* and results in the immensely sophisticated poems of Juan Ramón Jiménez— to name only one Spanish poet—being ignored entirely or characterized as "primitive" or "fake."

We had an Airedale that Jim was fond of. He found that if he sang in a high voice off-key, the dog would sing with him, probably in order to keep his eardrums whole, and the dog's singing delighted Jim. He put that Airedale in as many poems as he could. One evening we were in Madison probably visiting my Uncle Henry who believed all the flying saucers came from a large hole near the North Pole and who loved telling Jim about all that. We walked out near the water tower, and Jim wrote this poem, called "To the Evening Star: Central Minnesota."

> Under the water tower at the edge of town
> A huge Airedale ponders a long ripple
> In the grass fields beyond.
> Miles off, a whole grove silently
> Flies up into the darkness.

One light comes on in the sky,
One lamp on the prairie.

Beautiful daylight of the body, your hands
    carry seashells.
West of this wide plain,
Animals wilder than ours
Come down from the green mountains in the
    darkness.
Now they can see you, they know
The open meadows are safe.

When the Mysterious Hidden Woman, who is related
to Aphrodite and to Venus, arrives, human beings, as
I've mentioned, feel a trust in the natural world they
may not have felt since early childhood. In this poem
the sense that a large number of objects are not needed
for life, shows itself in the emphasis on one light:

One light comes on in the sky,
One lamp on the prairie.

The one star is Venus, of course, and that star is Hers.
We know the Mysterious Hidden Woman's connection
to seashells from Botticelli's *Birth of Venus*, if from no
other source. She calls human beings to long journeys.
The feeling of trust this time is put into the bodies of
animals, specifically wild animals, living in Wyoming
perhaps.

West of this wide plain,
Animals wilder than ours
Come down from the green mountains in the
    darkness.

> *Now they can see you, they know*
> *The open meadows are safe.*

He carried a small leather-bound spiral notebook with him always, in which he wrote often in a cramped musical hand. Inside the house he might carry on raucously, reciting a routine by Jonathan Winters about Elwood P. Suggins ("I was throwing some bags down there at the cement plant when I saw that flying saucer land in a wheat field—I think they must feed off wheat or something") or raving on about *Tristram Shandy* (whole sections of which he knew by heart), then take a brief walk, and ten minutes later all at once five or six lines, beautifully shaped by some invisible force, would appear in that little notebook. He would set down lines a number of times during the weekend. When he got to Minneapolis on Monday, he would type them up, and he had that abundance to work on the rest of the week.

We almost never read poems to each other until we had typed them and shaped them as best we could. Then it was a delight to read and to hear. We specialized in "cutting tails" off each other's poems, having discovered that the mind, when setting down a new thought or perception tends to say it once, then twice, and then a third time just to make sure the reader gets it. "Autumn Begins in Martins Ferry, Ohio" originally had about thirty lines; James frequently would cut off the last four or six lines from my poems. Chuang Tzu said something like, "Rain doesn't go on for days, and thunderstorms last only a short time. Why should human beings go on forever?"

James's models were clear. He had delighted for years

in the German of Trakl, which he came upon during his Austrian stay; he loved the Spanish poetry of Juan Ramón Jiménez, which he found in the marvelous green hardcover that H. R. Hays translated; the poetry of Antonio Machado, which he found first in Rexroth's booklet published by City Lights (translations James praised extravagantly again and again); Rexroth's own Sierra camping poems; and the Taoist poems in Robert Payne's anthology, *The White Pony*. He sensed by 1960 that a new poetry was possible in English that he could not have imagined in 1950.

His body and his psyche, and the relations between them, were complicated; and his being did not seem in any way a simulacrum of the poets he admired. He carried a great deal of anger in his neck and shoulders, and one would guess that Trakl carried that also, but James's landscape was industrial, in contrast to the agricultural landscape of the Spanish poets. Lorca longed for his childhood heart, but James's hatred of childhood tormentors was close to the surface. Finally, the ancient Chinese poets spoke of the world as a garden; by contrast he felt himself to be in a desert, "dying of thirst." One of his favorite passages from Goethe that he translated uses that image:

> *Oh Father of Love,*
> *If your psaltery holds one tone*
> *That his ear still might echo,*
> *Then quicken his heart!*
> *Open his eyes, shut off by clouds*
> *From the thousand fountains*
> *So near him, dying of thirst*
> *In his own desert.*

The Mysterious Woman both descends and ascends; the poet who serves Her must live both above and below, as the old Chinese poets continuously suggested. The poet's discipline lies in emphasizing the senses: movement of breath, sense of damp and dry, dusky light and clear light, sounds, odors—or a combination such as the rich sensory experience offered by a beehive. The Taoist brings the poem to the body. He does not do that because he is rejecting intellect or spirit; on the contrary the poetry is often ascensionist. But the conviction is that the ascension needs to be embodied: "As above so below." Abstract words can overbalance a poem on the side of ascension, let it float off without grounding, encourage the spirit to lose itself in the sky. Here is a passage James wrote in his notebook, a fragment from a longer poem, but one whole in itself. The poem respects the relaxed senses.

IN FEAR OF HARVESTS

It has happened
Before: nearby,
The nostrils of slow horses
Breathe evenly,
And the brown bees drag their high garlands,
Heavily,
Toward hives of snow.

It is not a great poem, and it is not meant to be. It is a moment when the legs of the bees laden with pollen lift toward the spirit-hive.

James wanted such embodied poems that traveled long distances, and he achieved them; of course, there were dangers too. In all poems that go out toward the edge there is the danger of sentimentality. This poem of James's he called "I Was Afraid of Dying":

> Once,
> *I was afraid of dying*
> *In a field of dry weeds.*
> *But now,*
> *All day long I have been walking among*
> *damp fields,*
> *Trying to keep still, listening*
> *to insects that move patiently.*
> *Perhaps that are sampling the fresh dew*
> *that gathers slowly*
> *In empty snail shells*
> *And in the secret shelters of sparrow*
> *feathers fallen on the earth.*

The opening four or five lines are clear and to the point. He says that Her arrival has made him less afraid of dying: the old Chinese poets said that many times. If death comes it won't be "dry," as he once feared it would be. The trouble in the poem begins after the word "insects." Once more the human feeling of adventure and fresh taste is given to creatures, but this time it doesn't work.

> *Perhaps they are sampling the fresh dew*
> *that gathers slowly*
> *In empty snail shells*

Well, the sarcastic mind says, maybe they are and maybe they aren't. I'm not saying this is a bad poem, but that it is walking just on the edge of the precious. The privacy that the Mysterious Woman brings with Her is given to the space under fallen sparrow feathers.

> And in the secret shelters of sparrow feathers
> fallen on the earth.

The image becomes "poetic" in the negative sense, too precious and too attenuated. He would have been better to claim the privacy for himself, rather than give it to snail shells and sparrow feathers, but we in the West have few examples in our own poetry on how to embody that energy. The Chinese poetry is skilled in such transfers, but it arrives in English translation without its music.

The Arabs felt that one had to meet all intoxicating energy with discipline, and the more intensity, the firmer the discipline needed to contain that without leakage. The Arabs asked for three disciplines I know of around Her: music, complicated forms in the poem, and meditation. The Provençal love poetry of the thirteenth century—more astonishing the more we study it—was all addressed to, written in the presence of, dedicated to, Her, and we know what intricate forms the Provençal poets used, adapted at the start from Arabic originals. We know, moreover, that the practice of such poetry required considerable musical accomplishment from those poets who ventured to speak of Her in public. The Arab and Persian poets made no secret of the prayer and religious disciplines, even to the point of asceticism, that the friendship with Her required.

She shouldn't be surprised, then, if certain adventurous poems in English written between 1959 and 1963 veer off, fall away from their centers, impute to animals what belongs to human beings, lose the shrewdness and containment we recognize in Taoist and Provençal poetry. The poets' surprise can become formless and generalized.

One day James and I were driving back to Minneapolis from a visit with Christina and Bill Duffy at their farm in Pine Island, Minnesota. Christina loved horses, had been a rider in Sweden, and continued to keep horses here. So horses were much on both our minds. Just south of Rochester, James saw two ponies off to the left and said, "Let's stop." So we did, and climbed over the fence toward them. We stayed only a few minutes; the ponies seemed to glow in the dusk and James felt that solidly. On the way to Minneapolis James wrote in his small spiral notebook, the poem he later called "A Blessing."

Just off the highway to Rochester, Minnesota,
Twilight bounds softly forth on the grass.
And the eyes of those two Indian ponies
Darken with kindness.
They have come gladly out of the willows
To welcome my friend and me.
We step over the barbed wire into the pasture
Where they have been grazing all day, alone.
They ripple tensely, they can hardly contain
  Their happiness
That we have come.
They bow shyly as wet swans. They love each other.
There is no loneliness like theirs.
At home once more,

They begin munching the young tufts of spring
  in the darkness.
I would like to hold the slenderer one in my arms,
For she has walked over to me
And nuzzled my left hand.
She is black and white,
Her mane falls wild on her forehead,
And the light breeze moves me to caress her
  long ear
That is delicate as the skin over a girl's wrist.
Suddenly I realize
That if I stepped out of my body I would break
Into blossom.

The munching of the young tufts is wonderful, as are many other images and sentences. In a few lines perhaps we feel some idealization. The two ponies were just ponies, and probably would have bitten one of us if we had stayed much longer without giving them sugar. The reader notices that one of the ponies is declared to be female, even though there was no evidence of that in the dusk. The feminine nature is insisted on: "she has walked over to me . . . ," "her mane . . . ," "her long ear"; and it is interesting to me that the whole scene takes place in the aura of the young feminine.

  her/long ear
  That is delicate as the skin over a girl's wrist.

Among those thoughts, in that mood, surrounded with that feminine presence, his anxiety over death is once more relieved.

Suddenly I realize
That if I stepped out of my body I would break
Into blossom.

The abrupt conclusion suggests two separate realizations: when he dies, he will not simply vanish or disappear, because the human body contains something invisible and strong that the reductive scientists do not speak of. Second, the Pauline and Augustine view that the body is corrupt, sinful, and utterly impure does not fit the experience. James imagines the act of stepping out of the body as complicated, stereoscopic, ascensionist. At one moment his image seems brilliant and sound, at another moment too hopeful and somehow ungrounded.

"The Blessing" remains an astonishing poem, able to move the reader into elegant discoveries. It is not a nature poem so much as a poem of longing. Michael Ventura has remarked that the poem says, "I wish this horse were a woman, I wish I were a horse, I wish I could step out of my body, I wish that this wishing could do some good."

As the sparrow and the pony poems suggest, there is some literary risk in welcoming the Mysterious Woman without the disciplines that the Arabs, among other cultures, brought forward in their welcoming. But there is considerable risk of failure in repeating the secular, dry, hard-bitten, Saturnian poetry also. If one's "expectant" poem becomes occasionally sentimental or overly naive, one can throw it away; the Saturnian poets need to learn to throw away many of their poems.

I have set down these poems and reminiscences to suggest that the Mysterious Hidden Woman is a secret presence in *The Branch Will Not Break* and a secret presence in the mood of that whole era. Her appearance contributed as much to the wildness of the sixties as the more adduced facts of the baby boom, the spread of television, the contraceptive revolution, the paperback revolution, the music of Elvis and Chuck Berry. Her presence shines inside the Beatles and She is the being who presides over Woodstock. As for Her complimentary being, Kali, or the Stone Mother, the Stones offered to supply that.

I'll close this little memoir with a glance at the two poems that James places last in *The Branch*—both, in my opinion, masterpieces. The first is "Milkweed." The scene is the farm: corn rows, the tall quack and pigeon grass, the farmhouse. When these outward objects have been mentioned and honored, the secret material begins. The Hidden Woman is described in some traditions as a treasure that has to be discovered. "I was a treasure that longed to be known."

MILKWEED

While I stood here, in the open, lost in myself,
I must have looked a long time
Down the corn rows, beyond grass,
The small house,
White walls, animals lumbering toward the barn.
I look down now. It is all changed.
Whatever it was I lost, whatever I wept for
Was a wild, gentle thing, the small dark eyes
Loving me in secret.
It is here. At the touch of my hand,
The air fills with delicate creatures
From the other world.

The Apocryphal book of *Wisdom* says of Sophia: "For within her is a spirit intelligent, holy, . . . unsullied, lucid, invulnerable, benevolent, sharp, irresistible, benificent, loving to people . . . pure and most subtle . . . she is so pure, she pervades and permeates all things."

One of the delights James had in the countryside around the farm, which he somewhere said that he loved "more than any other spot on earth," was that of walking in the fall along the ditches, plucking ripe milkweed pods, and then releasing their parachutes, each holding a single seed, onto the wind. It wasn't too good for the future of the Lundin field on the north side of the road, but one can't do everything right. The abrupt turn resonates perfectly with the old image of Venus or Aphrodite: She opens the soul to the other world.

> *At a touch of my hand,*
> *The air fills with delicate creatures*
> *From the other world.*

The final poem in *The Branch* is called "A Dream of Burial."

> *Nothing was left of me*
> *But my right foot*
> *And my left shoulder.*
> *They lay white as the skein of a spider floating*
> *In a field of snow toward a dark building*
> *Tilted and stained by wind.*
> *Inside the dream, I dreamed on.*
>
> *A parade of old women*
> *Sang softly above me,*
> *Faint mosquitoes near still water.*

So I waited, in my corridor.
I listened for the sea
To call me.
I knew that, somewhere outside, the horse
Stood saddled, browsing in grass,
Waiting for me.

The opening passage I'm sure describes an actual dream. Two fragments of his body, a right foot and a left shoulder, float in the air, somewhat like a spider thread strung out on the wind, over a snowy field and toward a mysterious dark building. So he is imagining his death of 1981 already in 1963. Or should we say that his old anxiety about death has taken form in these images? A chorus of old women offer some protection from above. The whole drama takes place, we learn to our surprise, in a corridor that leads toward the sea, and then the geography opens out to a strip of land near the sea. A horse is there, an animal stronger than a man, whose body is more powerful than the human body, and capable of longer journeys.

I knew that, somewhere outside, the horse
Stood saddled, browsing in grass,
Waiting for me.

The elaborate tenderness, calmness, trust, sensual immersion, and ascension that the Mysterious Woman repeatedly brings with Her forbid any simpleminded view of the poetry that springs up around Her. Some of the essays that tried to describe the poetry as a technique involving "the deep image" were so absurd that James did not think it worthwhile to answer them. There is a tendency in American criticism to reduce any new way of seeing the soul to a technique, such as "the deep image." She comes and goes as She wishes; the plant rises and falls to the earth; the blossom opens no one knows exactly when.

1988

David Ignatow
and the Dark City

I

David Ignatow has broken free of a naïveté so typical
of American poets. Whitman is his master, along with
William Carlos Williams, but he sees that Whitman's
insistence that we are all brothers, and friends, or should
be, will lead directly to murder and insanity.

> Let us be friends, said Walt . . .
> and cemeteries were laid out
> miles in all directions
> to fill the plots with the old
> and young, dead of murder, disease,
> rape, hatred, heartbreak and insanity . . .

To feel powerful and alive, we may want to hurt someone, or have evidence that our society is hurting someone in our behalf.

> How come nobody is being bombed today?
> I want to know, being a citizen

> of this country and a family man.
> You can't take my fate in your hands,
> without informing me.
> I can blow up a bomb or crush a skull—
> whoever started this peace
> without advising me
> through a news leak
> at which I could have voiced a protest,
> running my whole family off a cliff.

We are in the hands of a dangerous person when we read Ignatow—dangerous to that hopefulness and guilelessness hidden in us. He pulls out a knife, and we soon feel that the part of us that loves false comfort being wounded.

> Lovely death of the horse
> lying on its side, legs bent
> as in gallop, and firm policeman
> pointing his gun at the horse's head:
> dull sound of the shot, twitch
> along the body, the head
> leaping up from the ground
> and dropping—
> to hold me by its death
> among children
> home from school, the sky calm.
>
> Playfully, I note my grey head.

Do you trust doctors? Do you secretly believe the doctor is a wise father and you a child?

The patient cries, Give me back feeling.
And the doctor studies the books:
what injection is suitable for hysterics,
syndrome for insecurity, hallucination?
The patient cries, I have been disinherited.
The doctor studies the latest bulletins
of the Psychiatric Institute and advises
one warm bath given at the moment of panic.
Afterwards inject a barbituate. At this
the patient rises up from bed and slugs
the doctor and puts him unconscious to bed;
and himself reads the book through the night
avidly without pause.

Do you feel that we have made considerable progress—despite all the wars—in becoming civilized? Do you believe that we really do have a better grasp of certain ethical problems than the ancients had, that we have corrected certain excesses characteristic of primitive cultures or the Dark Ages?

At two a.m. a thing, jumping out of a manhole,
the cover flying, raced down the street,
emitting wild shrieks of merriment and lust.
Women on their way from work, chorus girls
or actresses, were accosted with huge leers
and made to run; all either brought down
from behind by its flying weight, whereat
it attacked blindly, or leaping ahead,
made them stop and lie down.

Inside human beings, then, there is a continual conversation between the primitive man, or primitive woman, and the civilized ego. How the primitive one behaves depends a great deal on the attitude the ego takes when they talk. Ignatow notes that if the civilized person insists on friendliness, the instinctive man or woman will be cold or hostile; if the civilized person is rational, the primitive man will be obstructive, chaotic, and barbaric. The primitive man may change the direction of his pressures and thrusts, even within the lifetime of the man, but he always clings as close as a shadow, the smell clinging "tenaciously through perfume and a bath." David Ignatow then is not writing trivial poems to fill up a book; you see in his poems a man in a fierce dialogue with Rousseau.

II

David Ignatow was born in 1914 in New York. He worked at his father's bindery shop on Lafayette Street in Manhattan for years, and ran the shop after his father died. He knows overwork, dealings, business, hiring and firing, paychecks, exploitation of others, disgust.

> *I see a truck mowing down a parade,*
> *people getting up after to follow,*
> *dragging a leg. . . .*
> *A bell rings and a paymaster drives through,*
> *his wagon filled with pay envelopes*
> *he hands out, even to those lying dead*
> *or fornicating on the ground.*
> *It is a holiday called*
> *"Working for a Living."*

A person suffers if he or she is constantly being forced into the statistical mentality and away from the road of feeling. Ignatow notices that the zoo is a good symbol for the statistical mentality, because the animal still has his instinctive Eros, but the Eros consciousness has nothing to hold to. A man is compared to a zoo lion:

> He gets up from the couch under the closed window
> and walks over to the rear wall
> where he lies down again upon a sofa
> as a change, as a protest.
> He has nothing to say, looks out at you,
> but then he might turn on his wife
> and tear her to pieces. It would
> extend the borders of his life
> and sex means nothing.
> For days he lies alongside the wall.

As we know, both capitalism and communism are shot through with disastrous conflicts, apparently built into each system, between Eros consciousness and the statistical mentality. Both cultures stumble into situations like Vietnam and Afghanistan and get stuck there by thinking in numbers. A shoemaker in the Middle Ages could be in business for years and remain in Eros consciousness, because he knew everyone who bought shoes from him, and he worked on a shoe long enough so that love-energy could flow into it, even for a short while. But it's clear that most business in the postindustrial era requires that Eros consciousness be given up and the love-energy pulled back inside.

> *The business man is a traitor to himself first*
> *of all and then no one else matters.*

By the time a businessman of that sort dies, he has passed far beyond the realm of Eros and is a partner of the grave, an entrepreneur of death itself.

> *I was last to talk to him*
> *or rather he talked to me*
> *and said, I've got a big deal on*
> *and want you in on it.*

In his hope and discipline Ignatow belongs to the group around Steichen and Georgia O'Keeffe—the artists who wanted to catch the frantic energy of New York, the sharp angles, steel and its brutal shadow, the negative cathedrals of business. Ignatow is one of our greatest city poets.

> *I'm in New York covered by a layer of soap foam. . . .*
> *The air is dense from the top of the skyscrapers*
> *to the sidewalk in every street, avenue*
> *and alley, as far as Babylon on the East,*
> *Dobbs Ferry on the North, Coney Island*
> *on the South and stretching far over*
> *the Atlantic Ocean. I wade*
> *through, breathing by pushing*
> *foam aside. The going is slow,*
> *with just a clearing ahead*
> *by swinging my arms. Others are groping*
> *from all sides, too. We keep moving.*
> *Everything else has happened here*
> *and we've survived: snow storms,*

> traffic tieups, train breakdowns, bursting
> water mains; and now I am writing
> with a lump of charcoal stuck between my toes,
> switching it from one foot to the other—
> this money trick learning visiting
> with my children at the zoo of a Sunday. . . .
>   And now what?
> We'll have to start climbing for air,
> a crowd forming around the Empire State building
> says the portable. God help the many
> who will die of soap foam.

Rollo May in his *Love and Will* maintains that more and more contemporary people are being possessed by the impersonal demonic, palpable now in great cities. "The most severe punishment Yahweh could inflict on his people was to blot out their names." David Ignatow's emotional range of feeling includes that terrible wiped-out-of-the-Book-of-Life feeling, the emptiness that invites demonic possession; he knows very well that he is capable of the violence that most poets attribute to "others." Doing violence is a way of proving that you can still affect others, and thereby do exist. Watching a man wash his car, Ignatow asks,

>   Is it
> the chamois cloth that stops him
> from killing the man and leaping
> upon the woman?

You know the president of your corporation, but the president does not know you. The only conclusion the unconscious can draw then is that you don't exist. Very few people are in touch with a private source of wildness inside them, let alone so close to it that they can confidently give the source of a name, as Socrates did, and as some Sufis, to mention a more recent group of "wild men," have done. What is meant by "mass man" in fact seems to be a state in which for large groups of people the private source of wildness is inaccessible. They have to look sideways then, to those around them, for assurance as to who they are.

Television news leads us to take in images of suffering, and then get used to seeing the images die the moment they hit the heart. Our feeling impulse wants us to stop the TV program, and relieve the suffering, and because it cannot, the impulse fades and dies. We all become objective and businesslike. If love-energy cannot coexist with the statistical mentality, death-energy can.

> *I have a big deal on*
> *And I want you in on it.*

David Ignatow is a genius in the subtle way he ties the death-energy to the most ordinary details of ordinary life. One thinks nothing is happening, but the implications are enormous. He makes a stark contrast with poets such as James Merrill or James Dickey, who talk of life-energy, but in some grandiose way that makes one ill.

III

Somewhere in all poetry that is alive, there are images of the knots of energy in the psyche that cannot be crushed. Some wild impulse urges the baboon, sent out as scout to protect the tribe, to leap on the jaguar, even knowing it will be killed. Some knot of energy encourages the ship captain to bring his ship in close to shore so that the "Secret Sharer" inside him can escape to land. That same impulse encourages the painter to leave his wife and children and go to some Pacific island, and tells the saint not yet a saint it will be all right for him to spend the rest of his life in a cave, and urges the worm to enclose itself so it can later become a butterfly. The dreamer falling is about to hit the earth, and the energy slips him sideways and flows away with him over the sea, and turns the sword into a transparent substance that can hurt no one, and allows a single hair to stir the sea.

> In the street two children sharpen
> knives against the curb.
> Parents leaning out the window
> above gaze and think and smoke
> and duck back into the house
> to sit on the toilet seat
> with locked door to read
> of the happiness of two tortoises
> on an island in the Pacific—
> always alone and always
> the sun shining.

Ignatow describes his foot as it rises and falls in a half circle while he lies in bed:

> its shape delicate, light,
> swift-seeming, tense and tireless

> *as I lie on a bed, my foot*
> *secretly a bird.*

He is open to the still larger community, larger than any nation. When Winston Churchill died, Ignatow remarked:

> *Now should great men die*
> *in turn one by one*
> *to keep the mind solemn*
> *and ordained,*
> *the living attend in dark clothes*
> *and with tender weariness*
> *and crowds at television sets and newsstands wait*
> *as each man's death sustains a peace.*
> *The great gone, the people*
> *one by one*
> *offer to die.*

It is astonishing that we should have produced in the United States a poet who can speak of community in this deep and convincing way.

He writes poems drawn up from the secret well of energy inside us, and yet he does not write narcissistic poetry. The recent emphasis on psychology has opened poets to the personal unconscious, which they assume to be private to them, as in the phrase "my dream." David Ignatow sees his dark side that way but also as reflected in the angers and frustrations of the community. For example, he sees it embodied in a stabber moving through a subway car. He is a poet of people who work for a living but he is also a poet of the greater community. Reading him, we experience in a deep way our union with the collective. His beautiful bagel poem suggests that he experiences his joyful side particularly as a member of the Jewish community.

> *I stopped to pick up the bagel*
> *rolling away in the wind,*
> *annoyed with myself*
> *for having dropped it*
> *as if it were a portent.*
> *Faster and faster it rolled,*
> *with me running after it*
> *bent low, gritting my teeth,*
> *and I found myself doubled over*
> *and rolling down the street*
> *head over heels, one complete somersault*
> *after another like a bagel*
> *and strangely happy with myself.*

IV

I'll close this essay with a brief look at a new theme that has appeared. Its mood is of swift, highly sustained desire. In Lorca the Eros impulse is felt by the reader to be absolutely indestructible—when Amnon looks at his sister naked on the roof, it's clear the desire he feels will have its way and break through all brush dams set in its path, whether by private conscience or collective rules. In Ignatow's poem "A Dialogue," a man wants to leap from a building to express his sorrow. He knows that people will try to block him. But he insists on his feeling, and he will have that, as Amnon had his desire.

I now will throw myself down
from a great height
to express sorrow.
Step aside, please.
I said please step aside
and permit me access
to the building's edge.
How is this, restrained,
encircled by arms,
in front of me a crowd?
I cannot be detained in this manner.
Hear me, I speak with normal emotion.
Release me
I would express sorrow in its pure form.
I am insane, you say
and will send me away—
and I will go
and die there
in sorrow.

Desire gets its way through the "third." Joseph Campbell writes often about the Western deadlock around opposites—communism versus capitalism, spirit versus matter, evil versus good, up versus down. Often a third thing the rational mind missed entirely enters and finds a new way.

No man has seen the third hand
that stems from the center,
near the heart. Let either
the right or the left prepare
a dish for mouth,

> *or a thing to give,*
> *and the third hand deftly*
> *and unseen will change the object*
> *of our hunger or of our giving.*

A great joy in reading his poetry is in experiencing again and again "the third."

David Ignatow has chewed over issues of right and wrong for years, relating unknown material coming in from below to questions of ethics. In a fine poem called "Rescue the Dead" he suggests that "loving" may be preventing us from breaking through to desire. The yearning for love is described as a forest with a secret grave in it.

> *To love is to be led away*
> *into a forest where the secret grave*
> *is dug, singing, praising darkness*
> *under the trees . . .*
> *Finally, to forgo love is to kiss a leaf,*
> *is to let rain fall nakedly upon your hand,*
> *is to respect fire,*
> *is to study man's eyes and his gestures*
> *as he talks.*
> *Is to set bread upon the table,*
> *and a knife discreetly by.*

We are each of us, he says, a part of the collective unconsciousness, and therefore we are unable to rescue the dead, who now live helpless in some vast consciousness, longing to be rescued. One of David

Ignatow's loveliest qualities is that he does not claim to be free.

> *You who are free,*
> *rescue the dead.*

1968, 1970, 1975, 1989

Hearing

Etheridge Knight

I had read Etheridge Knight for years, but never seen him. Then one summer I drove about six hours in the middle of the night to hear him read at eight in the morning, and when he finished I had the strangest sensation: I saw the applause blow right through his body, as mist blows through trees. Nothing held it. I had never seen anything like that.

I didn't know what it meant, and I still don't, but I understood that he wasn't operating from a defensive position, and his "ego" as we call the hungry-one-with-mouth-open wasn't opening out to catch and eat everything that went by. His "ego" hadn't claimed the achieved castle, as either builder or lord.

Some poems, like those of Wallace Stevens, are so marvelous in language that we don't care if they are true or not. The affectionate and warm language caresses the fur of the mind as young girls sometimes caress a cat, for minutes or hours on end. The language mind arches its back, goes into a trance, and doesn't care what is happening.

Other poems, equally marvelous, awaken the truth

receiver somewhere inside the body mind. We go into a different trance in which we expect truth, or perhaps, come out of our ordinary trance, in which we are inured to lies. How much sadness we feel because we have given up expecting truth. Every moment of our lives we exchange comfort or discomfort for statements we know are lies, or mostly lies, in gatherings with our parents, or at speeches, or watching a movie. How abandoned our truth receiver is: a bag-man, who spends the day without hope.

All of us who read Etheridge Knight know entire poems in which the truth receiver is able to live with dignity throughout the entire poem: "The Violent Space," "The Idea of Ancestry," the Hard Rock poem, "Cop Out Session," "Ilu, the Talking Drum," "Welcome Back Mr. Knight Love of My Life," "Rehabilitation and Treatment in the Prisons of America." I feel expectations of truth also reading Villon. . . . In Norman Cameron's translation Villon says,

> *I do confess that, after years*
> *Of anguish'd moanings and laments,*
> *Sorrows and agonies and fears,*
> *Labours and grievous banishments,*
> *I learned from all these chastiments*
> *More than from studying by rote*
> *That which Averroes comments*
> *On that which Aristotle wrote.*

and

> *I mourn the season of my youth*
> *(In which I revell'd more than most*

Before old age had brought me ruth).
Youth drank with me no final toast;
It did not march on foot, nor post
Away on horse: how did it go?
Suddenly in the sky 'twas lost,
And left no parting gift below.

I'll set down here three poems of Etheridge's. The first
is *the Idea of Ancestry:*

1

Taped to the wall of my cell are 47 pictures: 47 black
faces: my father, mother, grandmothers (1 dead),
    grand-
fathers (both dead), brothers, sisters, uncles, aunts,
cousins (1st & 2nd), nieces, and nephews. They stare
across the space at me sprawling on my bunk. I know
their dark eyes, they know mine. I know their style,
they know mine. I am all of them, they are all of me;
they are farmers, I am a thief, I am me, they are thee.

I have at one time or another been in love with my
    mother,
1 grandmother, 2 sisters, 2 aunts (1 went to the
    asylum),
and 5 cousins. I am now in love with a 7-yr-old niece
(she sends me letters written in large block print, and
her picture is the only one that smiles at me).

I have the same name as 1 grandfather, 3 cousins, 3
    nephews,
and 1 uncle. The uncle disappeared when he was 15,
    just took

*off and caught a freight (they say). He's discussed each
    year*
when the family has a reunion, he causes uneasiness in
*the clan, he is an empty space. My father's mother,
    who is 93*
*and who keeps the Family Bible with everybody's birth
    dates*
*(and death dates) in it, always mentions him. There is
    no*
place in her Bible for "whereabouts unknown."

2

*Each fall the graves of my grandfathers call me, the
    brown*
*hills and red gullies of mississippi send out their
    electric*
*messages, galvanizing my genes. Last yr / like a
    salmon quitting*
*the cold ocean-leaping and bucking up his birthstream /
    I*
*hitchhiked my way from LA with 16 caps in my pocket
    and a*
*monkey on my back. And I almost kicked it with the
    kinfolks.*
*I walked barefooted in my grandmother's backyard / I
    smelled the old*
*land and the woods / I sipped cornwhiskey from fruit
    jars with the men /*
*I flirted with the women / I had a ball till the caps ran
    out*
*and my habit came down. That night I looked at my
    grandmother*

and split / my guts were screaming for junk / but I
was almost
contented / I had almost caught up with me.
(The next day in Memphis I cracked a croaker's crib for
a fix.)

This yr there is a gray stone wall damming my stream,
and when
the falling leaves stir my genes, I pace my cell or flop
on my bunk
and stare at 47 black faces across the space. I am all of
them,
they are all of me. I am me, they are thee, and I have
no children
to float in the space between.

What could we say of this? It is not written from the
defensive position. The alertness to "the kinfolks" is
amazing. The "I" feels fully there. The sound is grand;
and the unexpected vowels carry the pitches up and
down with them as in old Anglo-Saxon poems:

monkey on my back. And I almost kicked it with the
kinfolks.
I walked barefooted in my grandmother's backyard /
I smelled the old
land and the woods / I sipped cornwhiskey from fruit
jars with the men
I flirted with the women / I had a ball till the caps
ran out

Like Anna Akhmatova, who inherits a literature of pain,
Etheridge Knight puts his pain on us but we don't feel

burdened by it. It is some kind of magic.
Here is the second poem, "Freckle-Faced Gerald":

Now you take ol Rufus. He beat drums,
was free and funky under the arms,
fucked white girls, jumped off a bridge
(and thought nothing of the sacrilege),
he copped out—and he was over twenty-one.

Take Gerald. Sixteen years hadn't even done
a good job on his voice. He didn't even know
how to talk tough, or how to hide the glow
of life before he was thrown in as "pigmeat"
for the buzzards to eat.

Gerald, who had no memory or hope of copper hot
*   lips—*
of firm upthrusting thighs
to reinforce his flow,
let tall walls and buzzards change the course
of his river from south to north.

(No safety in numbers, like back on the block:
two's aplenty, three? definitely not.
four? "you're all muslims."
five? "you were planning a race riot."
plus, Gerald could never quite win
with his precise speech and innocent grin
the trust and fist of the young black cats.)

Gerald, sun-kissed ten thousand times on the nose
and cheeks, didn't stand a chance,
didn't even know that the loss of his balls
had been plotted years in advance
by wiser and bigger buzzards than those

who now hover above his track
and at night light upon his back.

This talks about men raping men; it doesn't fall into the cliché that rape is done to subdue women; and he lets go all the talk of the rehabilitation, therapy, everything can be corrected, etc. As Robert Frost said when the wife slipped away from her husband in the garden and never returned:

> *Sudden and swift and light as that*
> *The ties gave*
> *And he learned of finalities*
> *Besides the grave.*

These poems are relatively early, but his poetry stays with truth. Five or six years ago he wrote a poem in the VA hospital in Indianapolis:

> *Former Sergeant Crothers, among the worst,*
> *Fought the first. He hears well, tho*
> *He mumbles in his oatmeal. he*
> *Was gassed outside Nice. We*
> *Tease him about "le pom-pom," and chant:*
> *"There's a place in France where the women*
> *   wear no pants."*
> *Former Sergeant Crothers has gray whiskers*
> *And a gracious grin,*
> *But his eyes do not belie*
> *His chemical high.*

> > Gon'lay down my sword 'n' shield—
> > Down by the river side, down by the river
> > side—

> *Down by the river side . . .*
> Grant Trotter's war was the south side
> Of San Diego. Storming the pastel sheets
> Of Mama Maria's, he got hit with a fifty
> Dollar dose of syphilis. His feats
> Are legends of masturbation, the constant
>   coming
> As he wanders the back streets of his mind.
> The doctors whisper and huddle in fours
> When Trotter's howls roam the corridors.
> We listen. We are patient patients.
>   Ain't gon' study the war no more . . . Well,
>   I ain't gonna study the war no more—
>   Ain't gonna study the word no more—
>   O I ain't gonna study the war no more.

I believe that Wallace Stevens and Etheridge Knight stand as two poles of North American poetry. Don't Mallarmé and Villon stand as two poles in French poetry? One doesn't have to choose and make one artificial, the other natural; one complicated; the other direct; one elegant, the other piercing. Nothing is as elegant as words that remain in truth. What do we expect of poetry?

1988

Denise Levertov:
With Eyes at the
Back of Our Heads

Reading Denise Levertov's best poems we sense water passing over some submerged stone threshold from one sea to another. Finally we are pulled down into deep water, and we begin to see a kind of phosphorescence in the deep sea holes:

> *the presence of a rippling quiet . . .*
> *draws the mind*
> *down to its own depths*
>
> *where the imagination swims,*
> *shining dark-scaled fish,*
> *swims and waits, flashes, waits and*
> *wavers, shining of its own light.*

Denise Levertov's first book was *The Double Image*, published in London in 1946. Already the words flow out across the line with a certain decisiveness that shows she is a born poet:

> *But there's an imagined numb indifference,*
> *a mockery, the beat of a dead heart,*
> *that sets a black seal on the open rose.*

Most of the thirty-seven pages of poetry in that book, however, are poetic in the bad sense of the word. The poems get completely tangled up in language like this:

> *Assiduously, like soft approaching nightmare,*
> *We amplify the sinister pretence*

The poems are visually foggy. The "I" feeling is uncertain. The poems talk of "we" things and "they" things: "We lie, dreaming of Europe" "A painted bird ... (is) all that stand between us and the wind." Kenneth Rexroth was the first American who took an interest in her work; in 1949 he included her in an anthology of contemporary English poetry he edited for New Directions. Among the poems he printed, there is one called "Folding a Shirt," which I have never seen printed elsewhere. She has found her way into her own poetry:

> *Folding a shirt, a woman stands*
> *still for a moment, to recall*
> *warmth of flesh*

It is clear she has broken through "we" to "I." It is interesting that in doing so she threw several things overboard. Poetry by English women has often had a gruesome and debilitating connection with upper- or upper-middle-class activities: Edith Sitwell's work is a good example. In her shirt-folding poem, Miss Levertov has jettisoned the upper-middle-class *situation*, and has already found her way into the world she will inhabit.

She waited nine years before she published her second book, a collection called *Here and Now*, which City Lights, no doubt at Rexroth's suggestion, published in 1957. The book is small, but strong. The mentality of the book is harsh, and the poems are free of the sentimentality that sometimes comes into her later books. Some of the harshness comes from an awareness of suffering. In some of her later poems, she will insist that she is more healthy than other people. In these early poems, she does not deny sickness:

> *Maybe I'm a 'sick part of a*
> *sick thing'*
> > *maybe something*
> > *has caught up with me*

She has a fine poem meditating on human energy:

> *It has no grace like that of*
> *the grass . . .*
> *it's barely*
> *a constant. Like salt:*
> *take it or leave it.*

She finally decides that what is valuable is the will to go

> *just that much farther, beyond the end*
> *beyond whatever ends: to begin, to be, to defy.*

The note of defiance is interesting. She is willing to break off her relationship to the reader cleanly—she demands nothing from him—and the poem possesses a fine independence. This book has a vigor, even a ferocity, that later softens as her poems show more desire to please the readers. I like the harsh ones.

She has two lovely poems on marriage here, one with that title, and a poem always fresh, no matter how often I read it, "Laying the Dust," about throwing water onto dusty ground.

Jonathan Williams a year later published her third book, a beautifully designed and printed collection called *Overland to the Islands*. Of all her books this one is the most influenced I think by William Carlos Williams. How that influence came about is curious. After World War II she met, in a Swiss hostel, an American writer named Mitchell Goodman, recently out of the U.S. Air Force. She later married him. It turned out that he had been a roommate of Robert Creeley's at Harvard and continued to exchange letters with Creeley. In those letters Denise Levertov found the excitement of new ideas. The whole series of events seem a strange coincidence, because looking back now, it appears that the ideas of Williams and Creeley are precisely what she needed to pull herself out of the soporific language of postwar English poetry. She later came to know Robert Duncan also, and he and Robert Creeley have been her guides, and Williams a kind of a second father. In *Overland to the Islands* the influence of Williams shows in the dash with which "vulgar" American speech is brought into the poem. The first words in the book are "Let's go," in a poem comparing a poet to a dog. In some lines describing marimba music:

> Somebody dancing,
> somebody
> getting the hell
> outta here.

One weakness her poems always have had and still have is that there are no real *ideas* in them, as there are ideas in Rilke's work or Yeats's. As a substitute for ideas, there are liberal *attitudes*, mostly taken from William Carlos Williams. For example, she begins a poem "Something to / nullify the tall women on Madison / sniffing, peering at windows, sharp-eyed, / the ones with / little hope beyond the next hat?" That sounds exactly like Williams. Williams influenced her in one other way. Williams was essentially a poet of pleasures—he loved to describe the way his car lights caught the green grass when he turned. In this book Miss Levertov also has poems that turn on pleasures—she describes going out to pick mushrooms with her mother in Wales, and as the mist lifts, suddenly catching sight of Snowdon Mountain, fifty miles away, or she describes the pleasures of seeing the colors of vegetables in a supermarket. Some poems close over a moving compassion—also visible in Williams—for old people, people whose bodies are abandoning them, who will have to stand naked soon before the sheer force of nature:

> And she: "Something hurts him in his chest,
> I think
> maybe it's his heart,"—and her's
> I can see beating at the withered throat.

The weakest poems are those in which she becomes objective like Williams, and sets to describing the outer world (the superhighway poem, for example, is rather weak); the strongest I think are those where she goes beyond Williams and begins to scare herself a little, as she does in "Sharks," "Action," and "The Absence." She goes downward in the mind, as Williams was rarely interesting in doing, and finds sharks:

> *For the first time*
> *I dared to swim out of my depth.*
> *It was sundown when they came, the time*
> *when a sheen of copper stills the sea,*
> *not dark enough for moonlight, clear enough*
> *to see them easily. Dark*
> *the sharp lift of the fins.*

We feel a little fear as she goes on in the next poem:

> *I can lay down my glasses . . .*
> *and walk*
> *right into the clear sea, and float there,*
> *my long hair floating, and fishes*
> *vanishing all around me.*

In 1960, New Directions published her next book, *With Eyes at the Back of Our Heads*. The poems in this book gleam with one of her greatest qualities: the marvelously crisp sound. A thicket of bristly consonants will suddenly give way to open vowel sounds that change themselves from "i" sounds to "o" sounds to "e" sounds, and then plunge back into harsh consonants again. The sound is exhilarating, and it expresses the emotional content of the poems perfectly. A good example is the closing lines of the title poem:

> the mountains we see with
> eyes at the back of our heads, mountain
> green, mountain
> cut of limestone, echoing
> with hidden rivers, mountain
> of short grass and subtle shadows.

To me the sound of these lines cannot be overpraised. They outdo any six lines of Williams in their decisiveness and far outdo anything of Marianne Moore's. Miss Levertov did not learn this powerful sound-music from Williams: it has always been in her work, it is a longing to fill fully the arms of the shirt of sound. She doesn't want her poem to "hang limp and clean, an empty dress." This cut or chiseled sound is at some different pole from the soupy rolling Swinburne sound and equally far from the prosy middle-of-the-road sound—half-open vowels, half-closed consonants—of most Williams disciples.

Miss Levertov works out another sort of sound in these poems—the sound of her own voice. Every voice has peculiar habits, its own way of doubling and redoubling on itself, which it accompanies with a certain sequence of pitches. Williams and Eliot both understood that getting your own voice into poems was something supremely important; Frost thought it was "the most important thing I know." In a country like the United States, where the sectional differences in voice are so pronounced, and add to the individual differences, poetry shoots off in all directions as soon as it becomes interested in avoiding echoes. That is good. Miss Levertov in *With Eyes at the Back of Our Heads* is consistently successful in evicting other people's voices. Of course, she has got rid of all recognizable meters too. In good "free" verse, all the supposed requirements of meter, of parallelism, of syllable count, of repeatable stanza, are shunned, so that the poetic conventions will be replaced by the poet's voice. It is a matter of taking the voice and distributing it among the words. Once the voice is on the page, the words are made to arrange themselves in such a shape that they can carry it. It is like making fifty mules arrange themselves in a barnyard so they can carry some weirdly shaped object that has ten or twenty arms on a body with a dozen right angles.

Let me quote first some lines by James Merrill in which we hear the "standard American (or English) voice":

> *How like a wedding and how like travelers*
> *Through alchemies of a healing atmosphere*
> *We whirl with hounds on leashes and lean birds.*

Miss Levertov says,

> *If I remember, how is it*
> *my face shows*
> *barely a line? Am I*
> *a monster . . .*

When her poems are weak there is usually a lack of vision. Rimbaud talks a great deal about himself and yet his poems have vision. What is the difference then between Rimbaud's landscape poems and Levertov's exotic Mexican poems? Rimbaud was always penetrating or pointing to something dismaying or at least incongruous within himself, even in his most exotic language. Trakl pierces to anguish about his failings even when he talks of Golgotha. But when Denise Levertov talks in many of the Mexican poems of outward things like superhighways and Mexican movies, and so forth, we have the feeling that she really *is* talking about these things.

Perhaps the best poem in the book is a curious prose poem, called "A Dream." The dream has two main characters, named Antonio and Sabrinus, who I think fundamentally represent two parts of the psyche, one more masculine, another more feminine. They are friends at the start, and their incandescent friendship warms the whole ship on which they live. Later, a storm comes. The poem is about some obscure psychic disaster that has fallen on the dreamer; this disaster is connected in some way with sexual jealousy or sexual anger at men. The two friends quarrel over a red boat, and luck leaves the ship. The dreamer sees them again years later in the hold of another ship, feverish, the two lie near each other ill and without radiance. It is a moving poem, and it retains the mystery of dream thought. A clear picture is used to talk of three or four things at the same time, and it probably talks of all of them accurately.

Her fifth book was *Jacob's Ladder*, published by New Directions only a year later. There are four or five good poems in the book, and two marvelous translations of Supervielle. Her characteristic strength comes through in the best poems: her soul goes out of herself, into an animal, for example. She can watch an animal lying down, and it is as if her human ego temporarily vanished: with sober eyes she looks, and the language becomes sober and serious:

> *The llama intricately*
> *folding its hind legs to be seated . . .*
> > *The llama*
> *rests in dignity . . .*
> *Those who were sacred have remained so,*
> *holiness does not dissolve, it is a presence*
> *of bronze, only the sight that saw it*
> *faltered and turned from it.*
> *An old joy returns in holy presence.*

At the same time, two weaknesses begin to appear—sentimentality and talkiness.

The sentimentality destroys some of the poems. It is not sentimentality about the poor, her troubles, dying rabbits, or sunsets, but rather sentimentality about words like "seraphic" and "demonic." Subway entrances become "steps to the underworld." In "From the Roof" she says, "who can say / the crippled broom-vendor yesterday, who passed / just as we needed a new broom, was not / one of the Hidden Ones?" Who indeed? In the rather prosaic life of these poems the truth is that a broom vendor is a broom vendor. A holy man becomes a holy man only by incredible physical sacrifice. Denise Levertov wants to have a prosaic housewifely life and find that her kitchen stepladder is Jacob's Ladder. It won't work. Her reading of the lives of saints is sentimental. They didn't see the muse in every butterfly. They took harsh steps, believed bitter things, drove wedges between themselves and the world, attacked their body, cared nothing about where they lived, developed schemes of physical humiliation and service to defeat and confuse their egos. But in "From the Roof" her emphasis is all on a bourgeois change of place.

> *By design*
> *clear air and cold wind polish*
> *the river lights, by design*
> *we are to live in a new place.*

The lines appear as the climax of the poem, they follow the mention of the Hidden Ones, who were supposedly disguised as broom vendors. She wants to draw out of the poem more spirituality in thought than she has put in in action. She wants to live as other people and then write as a mystic. That is impossible.

The second weakness—talkiness—is related to the first. A tone of wonder is assumed from the first word of the poem, and after that it is all talk. A good example is the blind man poem, called "A Solitude." It begins,

> *A blind man. I can stare at him*
> *ashamed, shameless. Or does he know it?*
> *No, he is in a great solitude.*
>
> *O, strange joy, . . .*

The instant of freshness lies entirely in the first stanza. After that she talks about how he doesn't care that he looks strange, how his voice is indifferent as one offers to help him, how the quiet of the blind man is different than the quiet of silent people, and so on. Rilke also has a poem on a blind man, and Rilke prepares explosions every two or three lines, astonishing images that no one could have thought of but a poet.

The talkiness now pervades many of the poems. A humorless egotism begins to enter also, and this no doubt contributes to the talkiness. In "Illustrious Ancestors" she tries to convince herself she is in a direct line from the mystic Angel Jones of Mold. In *Jacob's Ladder* she has a poem called "A Map of the Western Part of the County of Essex in England," where Essex is complimented for having sheltered her in her youth: "Roding held my head above water when I thought it was / drowning me . . . Pergo Park knew me . . ." and so forth. That is concealed self-praise.

Jacob's Ladder also contains "Matins," probably the worst poem Miss Levertov ever wrote. It contains two gruesome lines:

> *The authentic! I said*
> *rising from the toilet seat.*

There is a tone of triumph about the lines, as if she were Maria Callas singing *Aida*. Felix Pollak has written a substantial and very funny parody of this poem, all about the authentic in bathrooms. Felix Pollak's parody, which was published in *Smith* #6, ends,

> *The authentic! It rolls*
> *just out of reach, beyond*
> *running feet and*
> *stretching fingers, down to*
> *the green slope . . .*

No one should mock the seriousness of her search for the authentic, nor the fact that looking for it immediately around you is a more fertile mental effort than looking for it in sunsets or Platonic ideas. Still, there is a ponderous solemnity about it all, an utter lack of humor about herself.

In 1964 another large book, *O Taste and See*, came out,

Miss Levertov's weakest book. The talkativeness dominates now. The poems look like moth wings scattered around the lawn, somehow never able to find their bodies. The poems are pale, like leaves forced to come out of their buds too soon.

One unfortunate quality of the Black Mountain poets is artistic smugness. As a group they are positive they know exactly how poetry should be written today—the wise old men have told them—and all that is necessary now is to write more of it. Miss Levertov has said that she doesn't always agree with Olson's theories on breath, yet it is clear she pulls the whole Olson breath mystique around her as a protective shell. The refusal to rethink ideas comes about partly from the herd instinct of the Black Mountain group. At the slightest sign of danger, they lower their heads, paw the ground, and repeat louder: Break the line at the right point! Watch your breath! They resemble the preachers who, no matter what problem, practical or emotional, a parishioner brings to them, answer: Return to Christ! It is not easy to get through to a Black Mountaineer. If you say, this is not a poem, they say, "What do you mean it's not a poem? I broke the lines in just the right places for the length of my breath."

Besides the talkativeness, we notice something else happening in *O Taste and See*—a Victorian mist begins to overtake the book. For the first time, she refers to "the Muse" by name. The Greeks had the imagination to think up a name for this creature in their own lingo—Miss Levertov should follow their example. But the word "muse," like a Victorian chest, has become a status symbol. At one point she reports that "the Spirit of Poetry" ordered her to gather some "seeds of the forget-me-not'' for him. Apollo, Ishtar, and the Muse appear, not transformed at all, dressed in tattered clothes made from dust jackets of mythological textbooks; the poet treats them in a peculiarly solemn and humorless way, as if they were old family chairs or General Motors stocks. As a result, these wild gods become corny. For example,

> At Delphi I prayed
> to Apollo
> that he maintain in me
> the flame of the poem
> and I drank of the brackish
> spring there . . .
> and soon after
> vomited my moussaka
> and then my guts writhed
> for some hours with diarrhea . . .
>
> I questioned my faith . . .

It is probably Robert Duncan's influence that has brought in these pagan gods, but Robert Duncan has jabbing intuitions about what may have been going on with them, which Miss Levertov does not have. Because she has no ideas of her own about the gods, their names lie in her poems like inert stones.

The language in her next book *The Sorrow Dance* (New Directions, 1967) is increasingly Victorian, particularly in the smaller pieces.

Her energy however breaks through in several marvelous poems, "A Lamentation," "Remembering," "Second Didactic Poem," and two of the Vietnam War poems, "Life at War" and "What Were They Like?" In "Life at War" she talks about what it is like to live in a military state:

> The disasters numb within us
> caught in the chest, rolling
> in the brain like pebbles . . .
> We have breathed the grits of it in, all our
>   lives . . .
>
> Our nerve filaments twitch with its presence
> day and night,
> nothing we say has not the husky phlegm of
>   it in the saying,
> nothing we do has the quickness, the
>   sureness,
> the deep intelligence living at peace would
>   have.

All her strength, her depth of feeling, sound cut out like granite, her feminine compassion, the rhythm able to carry grief, the images that rise from far down in the mind, all come forward. The clear resonant words are set one next to the other like stones in a stream. In the war poems she is not a poetess among her subjects, winning easy victories over words; she is rather a human being facing her enemy, the Pentagon, who is stronger than she is. The result of this confrontation is not propaganda, but private poems whose movement is at times magnificent. The public work overturns our clichés about engaged work, being more private than her personalist poems.

This must be the end of a brief underground tour

through Denise Levertov's work. Her clinging so close to Robert Creeley and Robert Duncan has blocked her recent development. She appropriates wholesale practices of Duncan's, whether they fit her own intelligence or not. When she mentions Apollo, for instance, she doesn't know what she is talking about. She often sinks into self-deception. In this, her work is unlike Robert Creeley's, which is rocklike and unsentimental.

Despite the criticisms I have made, Denise Levertov is an absolutely genuine artist, in whose best poems words come alive by mysterious, almost occult, means. She does not think her way through the darkness of a difficult subject, she feels her way through the tunnel with her hair and the tips of her fingers that seem to give off light. When she comes back up into the daylight with the water she has found, it burns on the plate like pure alcohol, leaping up into the cold places.

1967

Thoughts on
W. S. Merwin

There is a poem supposed to have been written by Raftery, that Yeats liked so well:

> *I am Raftery the poet,*
> *Full of hope and love.*
> *My eyes without sight,*
> *My mind without torment.*
>
> *Going West*
> *By the light of my heart,*
> *Weary and sad*
> *To the end of the road.*
>
> *Behold me now*
> *With my back to a wall,*
> *Playing music*
> *To empty pockets.*

W. S. Merwin begins an early stanza this way:

> *I am a sullen unseemly man—*
> *Pray now no more for folly—*

> *Who in the bleak and tolling hour*
> *Walk like a chime without a tower,*
> *Rending a story, and complain*
> *Heartless and foolishly.*

We feel some lack of inwardness here. Or is it Irish jauntiness we miss? In Merwin's second collection, *Green with Beasts*, there is a poem describing a dreaming dog, with paws twitching, chasing tigers in a strange field. The poet imagines himself also standing there.

> *Strange even to yourself and loved, and only*
> *A sleeping beast knows who you are.*

This seems to me very powerful.

In another fine poem, "Low Field and Light," he feels himself lost, mysteriously drawn to some flat fields near the sea. He sees them as in a vision:

> *My father never plowed there . . .*
> *But you would think the field were something*
> *To me, so long I stare out, looking*
> *For their shapes or shadows through the matted*
>   *gloom, seeing*
> *Neither what is nor what was, but the flat light rising.*

In "After the Flood," he walks by the Hudson River. There is much description of flotsam, the swollen water, the altered shore, and so forth—the mysterious changes that have taken place suggest the possibility of sudden loss. Once he has fulfilled the need for describing the swollen and cruel river, he turns to something else.

I noticed
Near the bottom of the pack, just below
The highwater line, an old coat hanging
Snagged on a tree-branch, and caught myself
   wondering
What sort of drunken creature had passed there.

This comes suddenly alive because it is a genuine poetic image, not a mere description. There is also an inwardness in it; the poet senses deep inside himself that he might become that same sort of drunken creature.

He has written good poems about the coal-mining area of Pennsylvania where he was born. These poems exist in a real landscape and the people are vivid. One of the poems, called "Small Woman on Swallow Street" describes the sense of evil that seems to rise out of the hat brim of a Pennsylvania woman.

Four feet up, under the bruise-blue
Fingered hat-felt, the eyes begin. The sly brim
Slips over the sky, street after street, and nobody
Knows, to stop it. It will cover.
The whole world, if there is time. Fifty years'
Start in gray the eyes have; you will never
Catch up to where they are, too clever
And always walking, the legs not long but
The boots big with wide smiles of darkness
Going round and round at their tops, climbing.
They are almost to the knees already, where
There should have been ankles to stop them.
So must keep walking all the time, hurry, for
The black sea is down where the toes are
And swallows and swallows all. A big coat

> *Can help save you. But eyes push you down;*
>   *never*
> *Meet eyes. There are hands in hands, and love*
> *Follows its furs into shut doors; who*
> *Shall be killed first? Do not look up there:*
> *The wind is blowing the buildings-tops, and a*
>   *hand*
> *Is sneaking the whole sky another way, but*
> *It will not escape. Do not look up. God is*
> *On High. He can see you. You will die.*

The poem is cunning and strong. The evil in human nature is not related to Adam and Eve, or to theological doctrines, or to something the Greeks might or might not have done, but to kindly members of sewing circles in little towns in Pennsylvania, members of the poet's family, white Protestants. Other fine poems are "Grandfather in the Old Men's Home," and "The Drunk in the Furnace."

It is obvious that in such poems Merwin's poetic power, which is real, is coming up from underneath more and more powerfully. In the "Small Woman on Swallow Street," the written language gives way at times to a spoken language. The written language that is left does not kill the poem, but does dilute and weaken it tremendously.

In his poems and prose poems he sometimes gets down and wrestles with the images and, at other times, looks down on them from the high tower. When he does wrestle, the images, pressed by desperate need, break through and carry then a vigorous electrical charge, as if some toy were charged with four thousand volts. When he doesn't wrestle, we get the insistent generality, the general noun, "the gardener," "the sculptor," the constant air of a mystified countryside that is supposedly related to the collective unconscious. Objects and emotions float in space. That means the task of detaching them from their context has been done—Magritte does that too—but the writer has not always reattached them to a new content. Horseback riders appear before a castle at night, an old woman turns into a cat, you go to sleep in the attic and wake up in the cellar, and so on.

What I like about Merwin's work is the persistent energy, the willingness to set down the imperfect. He is of true help to those who are lonely, who sit reading to pass the morning. And I like the air of intelligence in the pieces, always ready to meet the unexpected, to find a tinker's house down in one corner of your room, or in the kitchen a message left by a glacier.

1960, 1978

In Praise of
Thomas McGrath

I

Their dream was that the war should
Go on forever.
　　And it hasn't stopped yet; one war or another . . .
　　And here's the first
Sellout from which the country is a quarter century sick.

Tom McGrath, when he describes the sources of the illness we now find visible all around us, does not go back to Johnson's failings, or Kennedy's ignorance, or back to the nineteenth-century galleys, but chooses a curious moment of time: the death of the labor movement, smothered under overtime during World War II.

At Paddy-the-Pig's then stand and drink the payday
　　cup . . .
　　　　　　　　"Slan leat!" says Paddy,
　　　　　　　　　Peers out
Of his internal Siberia (that's brightened by the eyes of
　wolves

*Only), "Down all bosses! After the war we'll get
  them!"*

*Ay. But the war got us first. Got the working class
By its own fat ass . . .*

Everything that happened during the McGovern cam-
paign—the crowds he met at the factory gates with
Nixon buttons, who complained that he wanted to give
amnesty to the "traitors," by which they meant the
protestors who had gone to Canada during the Vietnam
War—bears out McGrath's grasp of the facts.

*Still, hard to blame them. . . .
People who were never warm before napalm, who
  learned to eat
By biting spikes, who were bedless before
  Strontium 90
Hollowed their bones: the first war victims . . .
                        —in cost-plush cars.*

Tom McGrath is the only American poet whose poetry
helps you understand the gross, infantile, elephantine,
tantrum-throwing, brutal face of a labor leader such as
George Meany, his cigar stuck in his mouth like a pa-
cifier, roaring out greedy defenses of the American system, and insulting all Chinese workers as subhuman
beings who deserve to be wiped out. Not Merwin nor
Eliot nor Lowell nor Roethke help with the problem of
understanding this wild scene.

*Bugles!
  Parade!*

The mad generals are coming.
They are leading a captive,
A two headed falloutmade monster. . . .

And after the enemy passes the
patriots come:
Bespectacled professorial mass murderers all ivy
grown. . . .
A farmer carrying a pet pig: a pop artist
Palpitant on a field argent . . .

Tom McGrath can see, as many of our recent radicals
cannot, the connection between a pop artist and Meany.
. . . In McGrath you can see stated a perception about
recent events, which the New Age prefers not to enter:
he perceives a long grief come upon us, not allayed by
Mailer and Lowell's jocular appearances at rallies in
Washington cathedrals, nor comforted by Kerouac's
sentimental prose, a grief which Ginsberg's advocacy of
drugs for everyone in the fifties does not interrupt but
deepens . . . for Mailer, Lowell, Ginsberg, Kerouac are
all shoots from the wealth tree, which got so much fer-
tilizer during World War II and has shown such a fantastic growth record since.

But from that imagined hill I see also the absence of
light—
The abandoned farmhouses, like burnt-out suns, and
around them
The planetary out-buildings dead for the lack of
warmth, for the obscured
Light that the house once held.

So his work records, as the work of so many other artists of recent years does, some sort of a death, political and private at the same time. The next task then is to describe the process of rebirth.

When a person dies spiritually, he can be reborn in at least two ways. If we oversimplify, he can go on farther into his isolation and solitude, as Rilke did ... or he can be reborn by an inner communion with the group, a decided love of the community. Neruda took the last path as McGrath has.

> *We offered our bodies*
> *on the endless Picket Line ...*
> *Outlaws*
>   *system beaters*
> *While Establishment Poets, like bats, in caves with*
>   *color T.V.*
> *Slept upside down in clusters ...*

The question for us comes up: Who is "we"? Is there— if we take that route—a community with which we can have an inner communion?

McGrath has spent most of his life since fifteen as an active radical of the Left. He committed himself in the late thirties to a life outside the Establishment (at a time when the edges of the Establishment were a lot chillier than they are now), radicalized by a Wobbly who came to the North Dakota wheat fields when McGrath was nine. He was hounded during the McCarthy era and after. He is one of the finest documentary film makers in the United States and he was blacklisted in that profession all through the fifties and sixties.

For a man like that, who is "we"? Can he say "we"

to the Berrigans? Perhaps. Can he say "we" to the suburban radicals, such as Jerry Rubin, who used to declare
during the sixties that the white middle-class students
were "the most deeply oppressed of all"? The leftists
are too suburban. The energy of revolutions is energy
born in crushing physical labor—this is where the Revolution in Russia was born, as well as in China . . . such
energy is as strange to the seventies and eighties leftists
as horses were to the Aztecs.

The SDS leaders themselves understood that their attempt to organize the factories failed because the post–
World War II radicals were unable to include the working class in their "we."

The implication of McGrath's poem is that the post–
World War II radicals in looking for ideological links
with China and Cuba, looking for mental partners, have
failed to see that the United States has gone over the
hump—the so-called working classes have lost their
bodies and are now "heads" like the acid freaks and
with a similar craving for babyish comforts. The Revolution can take hold only in body people, or in people
who have given up head comforts, and have descended
again into their bodies.

If the radicals want a revolution, they would have to
become body persons and soul persons again. I leave
you to speculate on how they or we could achieve
that.

II

Poetry can be read for content, and I've tried to show
that McGrath's *content* can be found nowhere else in

American poetry. McGrath is not one of those who used to announce on billboards in 1970 "The War Is Over." The continuity of our wars stretches through each of us. As Lorca says, "A wire is stretched between the Sphinx and the safety deposit box which runs through the heart of every child who is poor." McGrath found that the only way to convey this complicated perception was to reenter the realm of the long poem. The problem he has struggled with is to find the right meter and tone for the long poem. It's clear that the poets of this century, in English especially, have been obsessed with the poem of 10 to 40 lines. McGrath belongs to the generation of Lowell and Berryman, and from his early stay in Baton Rouge, where Cleanth Brooks was teaching, he took on many New Critical ideas on the style and tone of poetry, as did most of his generation. His early poems are models of English-sounding rhyme, Donne paradox, and the language "tension" the New Critics liked in a poem. Both Lowell and Berryman at different points in their lives made attempts to break out of the Baudelaire-size poem. Lowell toward the end of his life attempted to make a long poem by linking together sonnets with the old New Critical particularity and tension. Berryman wrote a medium-size poem about Mistress Bradstreet. The poet who has thrown himself with the most energy into the problem of what a long poem today would look like is McGrath. His investigation is called *Letter to an Imaginary Friend*. In 1962 he published Part I, with about 3,500 lines—something over a hundred pages—then in 1970 finished Part II, so the poem, as published by Swallow Press in 1977 had a total of circa 7,000 lines. Three more parts have since been published adding about 3,000 more lines.

A 10,000-line poem brings up certain questions that the author of the 10-line poem doesn't have to answer. For example, "What will the meter be?" And surely one can't have a poem that long without "history" in it. All ancient poets put some "history" into their long poems, and Pound, in fact, remarked that an epic poem is a poem with history in it.

Some American poets have noticed an odd contrast: we live in an epical country, but the English language provides us models from only the lyric poem. For our literary heritage we rely on England, and it is a lyric country, if anything, certainly not—in the last thousand years—epic at all. So we have sonnet-size poems like the English ten-acre fields, separated from the universe by hedges. How can a sonnet be applied to the spaces of Montana where a single farm may include 40,000 acres? Robinson Jeffers tried to get space in by opening the poems vertically, sinking them into evolutionary wells, incest, and horse love. Sometimes he succeeded. The problem was that the petty details of American life, the interesting details of industrialized life, got left out.

Pound tried to do it by opening the poem up to medieval and ancient history. Huge sections of Italian history make their way in, and anecdotes from American politics are shoved in. In doing that, he fell out of personal touch with his own poem.

McGrath brings in history, not by reference to historical events lived by others, but by narrative. His success in making the narrative at home in Democratic–Republican English is not complete, but it is substantial. I'll set down here an example of McGrath's narrative from *Letter to an Imaginary Friend*, Part I.

That was the year, too, of the labor troubles on the
   rigs—
The first, or the last maybe I heard the talk.
It was dull. Then, one day—windy—
We were threshing flax I remember, toward the end of
   the run—
After quarter-time I think—the slant light falling
Into the blackened stubble that shut like a fan toward
   the headland—
The strike started then. Why then I don't know.
Cal spoke for the men and my uncle cursed him.
I remember that ugly sound, like some animal cry
   touching me
Deep and cold, and I ran toward them
And the fighting started.
My uncle punched him. I heard the breaking crunch
Of his teeth going and the blood leaped out of his
   mouth
Over his neck and shirt—I heard their gruntings and
   strainings
Like love at night or men working hard together,
And heard the meaty thumpings, like beating a grain
   sack
As my uncle punched his body—I remember the dust
Jumped from his shirt.
He fell in the blackened stubble
Rose
Was smashed in the face
Stumbled up
Fell
Rose
Lay on his side in the harsh long slanting sun

And the blood ran out of his mouth and onto his
  shoulder.

Then I heard the quiet and that I was crying—
They had shut down the engine.
                    The last of the bundle-teams
Was coming in at a gallop.
                        Crying and cursing
Yelled at the crew: "Can't you jump the son-of-a-bitch!
Cal! Cal! get up"
But he didn't get up.
None of them moved.
Raging at my uncle I ran.
Got slapped,
Ran sobbing straight to the engine.
I don't know what I intended. To start the thing
  maybe,
To run her straight down the belt and into the feeder
Like a vast iron bundle.
I jammed the drive-lever over, lashed back on the
  throttle,
And the drive belt popped and jumped and the thresher
  groaned,
The beaters clutched at the air, knives flashed,
And I wrestled the clutch.
                    Far away, I heard them
Yelling my name, but it didn't sound like my own,
And the clutch stuck. (Did I want it to stick?) I
  hammered it
And the fireman came on a run and grabbed me and
  held me
Sobbing and screaming and fighting, my hand clenched

On the whistle rope while it screamed down all of our
  noises—
Stampeding a couple of empties into the field—
A long, long blast, hoarse, with the falling, brazen
Melancholy of engines when the pressure's falling.

Quiet then. My uncle was cursing the Reds,
Ordering the rig to start, but no one started.
The men drifted away.

                              The water monkey

Came in with his load.

                              Questioned.

He got no answer.
Cal's buddy and someone else got him up
On an empty rack and they started out for home,
Him lying on the flat rack-bed.

Still crying, I picked up his hat that lay in the churned
  up dust,
And left my rack and team and my uncle's threats,
And cut for home across the river quarter.

III

Thomas McGrath has created his poetry out of the
old love of conflict that invigorated literature until the
universities shut it down in their search for deodorized
and vinyl-coated tax dollars. That's one way McGrath
might describe the change. We all see the new Yuppie
flatness in the verse world, which amounts to muzzy
mouthings about archetypes and grandfathers but nothing said about late capitalism, exploitation of trees, or
opinions that infuriate the settled. Why should opinion

have disappeared from poetry? Yeats built his founda-
tions on opinion. His opinions on the occult, on the
value of Anglo-Irish aristocracy, on ghosts, on cycles of
history make the polite scholars uncomfortable to this
day. Or is it the readers who want poetry that is free of
opinion? In any case we get what Donald Hall has called
the McPoem, fast-food verse, packaged the same in all
states, free of anger, made from contented steers.

McGrath wrote a poem called "Blues for the Old Revolutionary Women"—for Mother Bloor, Mother Jones,
Meridel Le Sueur." He says of these women:

> *What is simple virtue can never be denied,*
> *Explained, or cancelled. Still, it is not*
> *Enough to love a world that must be changed.*
> *This was the earliest thing they learned.*

Loving the world is not enough. The world asks—in
order for each person to become human—for conflict,
fierceness, opinions, strikes, demonstrations, causing
trouble.

McGrath incorporates in his wild poems most of the
rhetorical flourishes and high jinks possible in English.
During an interview in the eighties, McGrath attacked
William Carlos Williams for dismantling the rhetorical
English car that Shakespeare, Dickinson, Milton, Hopkins rode in. Williams substitutes in effect a sort of boy's
wagon, good for hauling cats or chickens. Many poets
considered this interview to be outrageous, because we
are supposed to regard Williams as a saint. "So much
depends upon / the red wheelbarrow . . ." So much depends on complicated thinking, elaborate syntax, many-
layered words, non-chickens.

McGrath shows an immense range of language. Hairy words sit down next to shiny words, scholarly words next to groovy words.

> And between the new macadam and the Scalp Act
> They got him by the short hair; had him clipped
> Who once was wild—and all five senses wild—
> Printing the wild with his hoof's inflated script
> Before the times was money in the bank,
> Before it was a crime to be so mild.

Language is the greatest gift of our ancestors and we need to keep words like "transfiguration" as well as "bread" and "yeast."

> On the Christmaswhite plains of the floured and
>   flowering kitchen table
> The holy loaves of the bread are slowly being born:
> Rising like low hills in the steepled pastures of light—
> Lifting the prairie farmhouse afternoon on their arching
>   backs.
>
> It must be Friday, the bread tells us as it climbs
> Out of itself like a poor man climbing up on a cross
> Toward transfiguration.
>   And it is a Mystery, surely,
> If we think that this bread rises only out of the enigma
> That leavens the Apocalypse of yeast, or ascends on the
>   beards and heads
> Of a rosary and priesthood of barley those Friday
>   heavens
> Lofting . . .

> But we who will eat the bread when we
> come in
> Out of the cold and dark know it is a deeper mystery
> That brings the bread to rise:
> it is the love and faith
> Of large and lonely women, moving like floury clouds
> In farmhouse kitchens, that rounds the loaves and the
> lives
> Of those around them . . .
> just as we know it is hunger—
> Our own and others'—that gives all salt and savor to
> bread.
>
> But that is a workaday story and this is the end of the
> week.

IV

McGrath's generation of poets is a strong generation, which includes many excellent poets. I think of Elizabeth Bishop, Robert Lowell, John Berryman, Karl Shapiro, Richard Wilbur, Delmore Schwartz, Randell Jarrell, William Everson, David Ignatow, and Thomas McGrath. In terms of fame, the last names are the surprises, but their work, I'm sure, will last.

McGrath has many moods besides the narrative and political poems that make use of the full range of English rhetoric. A simpler mood we can feel in the group of poems written for his son Tomasito.

> My little son comes running with open arms!
> Sometimes I can't bear it,

Father.
Did I, too,
Open your heart almost to breaking?

("Poem")

And he remembers his father. Tom McGrath, born in
1917, would have been twelve when the Depression fell
on the farmers.

Father, you must have been,
Like now—
On a tiny raft while the big ship went down.

You had taken our mother aboard
While the decks were still awash.
Then, for a little time, it must have seemed almost like
    heaven—
Though you've never said that
In words.
Nor has she
            but I saw it
In both your eyes when you thought
We were not watching.

Heaven, then.
Even on the dark and shoreless waters.
Other rafts went down. Around you cries
Went up—
            agonies—
Sharks clouding and clotting in the sea—
Heaven.

Then our mother began
Presenting us to you:

♦ 143 ♦

One, every couple of years,
Was conjured out of the gypsy tent of her black skirts.
And you fed us:
Fishing all night in the hungry waters,
Giving your clothing to warm us,
And you naked, shivering in the cold,
                                        enduring—
Why didn't you drown us like a litter of sick cats?
But . . . didn't.
You gave your freedom for our mother's fulfillment.
And you gave us
All the lost honey of a young man's years—
Steering through the vicious seas of those bitter
    times . . .
Ah . . . dearest father, dear
Helmsman!

                                        ("Offering")

V

Finally I want to praise McGrath's ability to eat grief.
Here are the final lines of his poem on the soldiers who
died in Korea. He regards the Korean War from a political point of view and yet when he thinks of the men
who died there, his emotion is that of pure grief resembling some of the old Greek elegies for men fallen in
battle.

Wet in the windy counties of the dawn
The lone crow skirls his draggled passage home:
And God (whose sparrows fall aslant his gaze,
Like grace or confetti) blinks and he is gone,

And you are gone. Your scarecrow valor grows
And rusts like early lilac while the rose
Blooms in Dakota and the stock exchange
Flowers. Roses, rents, all things conspire
To crown your death with wreaths of living fire.
And the public mourners come: the politic tear
Is cast in the Forum. But, in another year,
We will mourn you, whose fossil courage fills
The limestone histories: brave: ignorant: amazed:
Dead in the rice paddies, dead on the nameless
    hills.

("Ode for the American Dead in Asia")

There are four lines of McGrath's that unite many of his themes: his desire to travel long distances, his excursions into history, his courage and the way he exhorts others to courage, and finally his adult comprehension that life is grief and we need to learn how to digest that grief joyfully.

EPITAPH

Again, traveller, you have come a long way led by that
    star.
But the kingdom of the wish is at the other end of the
    night.
May you fare well, companero; let us journey together
    joyfully,
Living on catastrophe, eating the pure light.

1987

Robert Lowell's
Bankruptcy

The major older poets have all died in the last years; the publishing world feels lonesome without a great poet around. Robert Lowell is being groomed for this post. The result is evil, especially for Lowell. Mr. Lowell has written powerful poems in the past, and some good poems at all times, but the last thing we need is another review trying to show he is a master.

Most of the poems in *For the Union Dead* are bad poems. Everyone writes bad poems at times, but advice from other poets is often a great help in keeping the worst of them from being published. Eliot, as everyone knows, sent *The Wasteland* to Pound. Pound also helped Yeats. Poets' criticism is harsh. Lowell seems to get none of it. He is surrounded by flatterers. Moreover, one has the sense that many of the bad poems in the book were written to satisfy demands—the demands of people like Jason Epstein, Stephen Marcus, and A. Alvarez, perfect examples of the alienated Establishment intellectual, none of whom knows anything about poetry. Lowell's vision of himself seems more and more to be identical with that of the people around him.

As we read *For the Union Dead*, we realize that two intellectual traditions, both bankrupt, have come together in the book. One is the entire string of intellectual longings represented by the history of the *Partisan Review*. The *Partisan Review* writers never broke through to any clear view of modern literature or politics. Their insistence on the value of alienation, their academic notions of modernism, are dead, like fatigued metal.

Phillip Booth foolishly compared Lowell to Whitman in his review, but Lowell's book embodies exactly what Whitman was fighting against. *For the Union Dead* has a peculiarly stale and cold air, instantly recognizable. It is the air of too many literary conversations, an exhausting involvement with the Establishment.

Because the ideas behind the book are decrepit, Lowell has no choice but to glue the poems together with pointless excitement. The persistence of bodiless excitement derives from a second bankrupt tradition, which is centred on the notion that an artist must never be calm, but must be *extreme* at all costs. This destructive notion, a bourgeois notion, flows from both right-wing influences on Lowell, like Tate, and left-wing influences like the *Partisan Review* writers.

Lowell has always had a poor grasp of the inner unity of a poem. In *Imitations* he often inserted violent images into quiet, meditative poems—his translations of Montale, for example—without realizing that the sensational images had destroyed the inner balance of the poems. In *For the Union Dead* he does the same thing to his own poems.

The routine violence in Lowell's poems reminds one of nineteenth-century provincial literature.

> *The pitying, brute, doughlike face of Jael*
> *watched me with sad inertia, as I*
> *read—*
> *Jael hammering and hammering her nail*
> *through Sisera's idolatrous, nailed head.*

For the Union Dead is something rare, a book of poems that is a melodrama.

The attempt to glue the poems together with mere excitement fails. Time after time, Lowell sets out in a poem to live inside a certain emotion, and suddenly a flood of objects buries the whole project. In seven poems, "The Mouth of the Hudson," "The Old Flame," "The Flaw," "For the Union Dead," "Water," "Fall, 1961," and "Night Sweat" the inner and outer worlds hold together, sometimes for only a few lines, sometimes for the whole poem. But the rest of the poems are melodrama; the inner and outer worlds have split apart.

Men write melodrama when the ideas available to them are dead. Lowell tells us that modern life makes everyone nervous, that we shouldn't support South American generals, that gods seem less real as we grow older. The ideas Eliot and Stevens put in their poems had size and vigor; Lowell's ideas are banal and journalistic. They have no life of their own, and are painfully incongruous in poems intended to be on the highest level.

The question we have to ask about the book is not why there are a few good poems—there are good poems because Lowell's talent is very great—but why so many incredibly bad poems appear in the book. Moreover, they are an odd sort of bad poem. When Eliot and Stevens wrote bad poems, these were weaker versions of their good poems, but Lowell's bad poems take on the quality of lies.

> *Perseus, David and Judith,*
> *lords and ladies of the Blood,*
> *Greek demi-gods of the Cross,*
> *rise sword in hand*
> *above the unshaven,*
> *formless decapitation*
> *of the monsters, tubs of guts,*
> *mortifying chunks for the pack.*

This is like a bishop lying about the early history of the church to a half-literate audience. If Lowell were to say these transparent pedantries in a more modest tone, it wouldn't be so offensive. It is the air of grandeur he puts on when he writes this empty rhetoric that is so offensive. The passage is coarse and ugly. Even worse, it is unimaginative.

> *Horrible the connoisseur tyrant's querulous*
> * strut;*
> *an acorn dances in a girdle of green oak*
> * leaves*
> *up the steps to the scaffold to the block,*
> *square bastard of an oak.*

What Lowell is doing here is counterfeiting. He is counterfeiting intellectual energy, pretending to be saying passionate things about tyrants and hangings, but in fact he gives only a series of violent words set next to each other; the indignation is ersatz, and the passage means nothing at all.

By and large, *For the Union Dead* is a counterfeit book of poetry. Lowell is pretending to be at the center of himself, when he is not. He is pretending to have *poetic* excitement, when all he has to offer is *nervous* excitement. And that is accepted as poetry, for American readers are so far from standing at the center of themselves that they can't tell when a man is counterfeiting and when he isn't.

The people who praised this book so highly did no one a service. Something evil is happening to Lowell: he is being praised for what is not in his books. We and Lowell are being presented with a false vision of his poetry. This cannot help but draw him farther from himself.

1966

Louis Simpson and
the Face of the Unknown

I
THE FACE OF HISTORY

Louis Simpson's poems are deeply aware that their author lives in one age and not in another. Everywhere in Louis Simpson's work there is a sense that an era of some sort has come to an end:

> O the ash and the oak willow tree
> And that's an end of the infantry! . . .
>
> Collect yourself. Observe,
> It's nearly day . . .
> Concrete and cactus are the real
> American tragedy.
> We should collect our souvenirs and leave.

The people in his poems interest me—St. John the Baptist, Anthony, Mary Magdalene. Girls and women seem to take a larger part in his book than in many books of poems. Most of the male poets of our generation are like Ulysses, tied to the mast to keep them from yielding too much to women, and they sail on to the Ithaca of their art, pure but somewhat stiff from being bound by ropes. Mr. Simpson is more at home in this world.

His poetry has a wry and compassionate view of people, which does not exclude humor or tenderness. There is a magnificent poem in his first volume, *Arrivistes*, called "Rough Winds Do Shake the Darling Buds of May." The second stanza reads,

> *She is sixteen*
> > *sixteen*
> > > *and her young lust*
> *Is like a thorn*
> > *hard thorn*
> > > *among the pink*
> *Of her soft nest.*
> *Upon the thorn she turns, for love's incessant sake.*

Later he describes a woman with one line:

> *Noli me tangere was not her sign.*

The third thing that interests me are his poems about the war. Surely "Carentan O Carentan" in *Arrivistes* is the best poem written yet about World War II by any generation. It does not seem the poem of a spectator, but a participant. "Arm in Arm" and "Alain Alain" in that book are also extremely good, as well as "Memories of a Lost War" and the magnificent "The Ash and the Oak" in the later book. The war described in his poems could never be any other war than World War II. It is not "war itself" but a specific battle, which, in a mysterious way, seems already imagined in the long train of crusades, sieges, and battles over one thousand years, of which it is a part. As we read his poems, the events of the West appear, as if by surrealist means, as a sort of mirage in our minds; we glimpse a battlefield here, a tower there, some crusaders, now a Roman legion, a fop of Louise XVI, now vast armies, now a man eating locust. In short, his subject matter is partially the history of the West.

He has written a long narrative poem about World War II called "The Runner." It gives the impression of a great depth, brought up into rather awkward poetry. Despite that, the writing has genuine power. Judson Jerome has suggested that we are never far from hallucination in Mr. Simpson's poems—and it is true that his descriptions often seem hallucinatory. I will quote a passage from "The Runner." An American infantry company is on the front near Bastonge in 1944. It is winter. The Americans are retreating. There have been rumors all night that the company is being left to face the Germans alone. Suddenly near dawn, the German tanks appear.

> At the foot of the slope
> The trees were shaking, parting. There emerged
> A cannon barrel with a muzzle-brake.
> It slid out like a snake's head, slowly swinging.
> . . . The tank was growing large.
> The cannon flashed. Machinegun tracers curved
> Toward it, and played sparkling on the steel.
> Still it came on, glittering in return
> From its machineguns. Then, a crashing flame

> Struck it, leaving a trail of smoke in air.
> The tank shuddered. It slewed broadside around.
> Inside the plates, as on an anvil, hammers
> Were laboring. It trembled with explosions,
> And smoke poured out of it.
> The slope was still,
> Sprawling with hooded figures—and the rest
> Gone back into the trees. Then there began
> The sound of the wounded.

The writing is very strong, but we could say that its power lies in its visual imagination, not in the rhythm or diction. It is as if one were sitting in a sunlit room with clouded windowpanes. The strength comes from the sun, but the light is dimmed. The rhythm, reminding one of Wordsworth, clouds the pane, and the diction, which is neither unusual nor inadequate, but more or less what one would expect, also dims the light. The poet is describing new experiences and inner sensations, for which there is no extensive precedent in English poetry, with a rhythm and diction developed in another century for totally different moods and events. Because the poem is divided against itself, a prosiness comes in. This division is a profound problem for all poets: we have many new experiences and no real way to write about them. The older poetry of the sonnet is of very little help.

Embarking on a poem with such an intractable subject matter, a poet might decide not to do it at all—or to wait twenty years hoping he will have an appropriate line by then. Mr. Simpson chose to write it now, using whatever form seemed to him most appropriate. The poem fails, but this failure is worth many successes.

In Mr. Simpson's work generally one is surprised by the appearance of unpleasant public realities such as World War II and the gas chambers. There is one reason I think so highly of Louis Simpson; there is a great reluctance among poets recently to bring such subjects into poetry. Writers such as James Merrill, for example, would never think of it; his idea of poetry does not include long wars. There is a fine Simpson poem called "The Bird." In this poem, a gentle German who always sings, "I wish I were a bird," takes up duties at a concentration camp for Jews.

> *"You'll never be a beauty,"*
> *The doctor said, "You scamp!*
> *We'll give you special duty—*
> *A concentration camp.*

But Heinrich learned:

> *"Ich wünscht, ich wäre ein*
>   *Vöglein,"*
> *Sang Heinrich, "I would fly . . ."*
> *They knew that when they heard him*
> *The next day they would die.*

When the Russians liberate the camp, the Nazi is nowhere to be found. He has evidently turned into a bird, for the Russian colonel, writing his report, sees a small bird singing outside in a tree. I am very interested in these strange shifts of reality. In another poem, an American soldier dreams he is in Paris during World War I. Looking up, he sees two old biplanes fighting and realizes he is a French soldier and that some long-dead French soldier fought through World War II in his uniform. Mr. Simpson's poetry at times is like a man who sits in a living room quietly talking, and gradually smoke begins to come out of his ears, and to gather over his head. This sudden shift from one kind of reality to another seems to me one of the major qualities of his poems.

I am also interested in the poetry about America. "America is old." "We were the first to enter on the modern age." "American begins antiquity." Mr. Simpson treats America somewhat as the Russian writers treat Russia—they talk about their country and give what ideas they have. Mr. Simpson offers the metaphor of "pure space" for America—where there is nothing but an infinite freedom to look. Lacking any monuments of grief or suffering, the land remains wild or inhuman.

> *The country that Columbus thought he found*
> *Is called America. It looks unreal, . . .*

But man came:

> *And murdering, in a religious way,*
> *Brings Jesus to the Gulf of Mexico.*

His poetry is in one sense the opposite of the poetry of Jiménez, who wanted his poetry to be "all present and no history." Mr. Simpson insists that the past be somehow in the poem.

The first poem in *A Dream of Governors* is a short history of the West from pastoral Greece to the present. The recent growth of the secular powers, such as America, greeted with such cries of joy from Hillyer, Ciardi, and the other poets of the Uplift, is described in this way:

> Old Aristotle, having seen this pass,
> From where he studied in the giant's cave,
> Went in and shut his book and locked the brass,
> And lay down with a shudder in the grave.

Louis Simpson's poetry, unlike some optimistic verse of the forties, has a darkness and a suffering, without any schemes to avoid them.

He sometimes gives the impression of laziness, for he chooses, as I've mentioned, any form that will do, just as people going to the front commandeer any old car, and at other times, the impression of genuine thoughtfulness and artistic integrity. In his tragic feeling he is virtually alone in his generation.

II
THE FACE OF THE UNKNOWN

Louis Simpson has always had a major gift for the image with unconscious ingredients: "the drugstore glows softly, like a sleeping body." In *Searching for the Ox*, he lets that sort of image lie. He's tired of that. He's going to let others do it; there are lots of imitators paddling on the waters of the unconscious in small kayaks. He's gone off on a tack this time, alone, I'll try to describe that tack, as I understand it from this book.

Couldn't we say that images, when used by a genius, make up a kind of living face of the unknown? We are quietly watching that face as we read a poem; all at once

the face opens an eye unexpectedly, and we shudder
... for somewhere inside, a face responds to that. An
eye in us opens. So a group of images can convey from
one person to another the expression on the face of the
unconscious as it turns.

How many other faces does the unconscious have?
Well, the Sufis use funny stories as a face, and they
work. By "work," I mean they bypass the defenses of
the overcivilized mind and penetrate to our living intelligence instantly. Music is a sort of mask or face ...
sometimes so well fitted that we weep hearing it, probably at the same places the composer wept. The occult
theories of alchemy make a face. And there is another
face few people think of—the ordinary details of daily
life ... I mean the details that actually happen. Simpson
decided to stake his book on these. After all, if the unconscious is truly powerful, why shouldn't its secret face
be visible in the banal details of daily life? Do we think
the unconscious is so weak it can only influence the
mind of surrealist poets? It must also influence the
choice of records a drunk puts on just before he falls
asleep; it must influence the sounds a man hears after
coming back from a date with a woman who is still
attached to her parents; it must influence what the movers do when they come to cart away furniture from a
house after a divorce. (In the last instance, Simpson
says, the movers tore up the poster of Adlai Stevenson
and burned it in the fireplace, put African drums on the
stereo, and went stomping around.)

Every detail in the poem "Baruch" is ordinary. I think
"Baruch" is a masterpiece, so I'll concentrate on it as an
example of the best poems in the book. One of the
greatest qualities human beings have is longing—long-

ing for spiritual labor. "He wishes to study the Torah." In the world of consciousness, a division so many humans have experienced is the conflict between the longing spirit and the banal details of working for a living, raising children, talking each day with a wife or a husband. "He wishes to study the Torah / But he has a wife and family." Apparently the unconscious wants human beings to experience more of the unknown, whether it is the undiscovered ocean and its terrors—as in Melville—or the weirdness of the edges of the mind-area, as in parapsychology. But for such discovery we need training, or the unknown can kill us.

All of this is said in the first section of "Baruch." Baruch could not give in to his longing to study the Torah because he owned a dress-hat factory. One night it burns down. That detail is right, and Melville and Hawthorne would agree. An event in the physical world hides behind it a spiritual truth. Fire can intervene between heavy earth details and the lightness of spirit—perhaps fire is the only way to move from one to the other. So, when fire takes his business, Baruch, relieved, gives himself to the Word:

> And he did from that day on,
> reading Rashi and Maimonides.
> He was halfway over the Four Mountains
> when one day, in the midst of his studying,
> Lev Baruch fell sick and died.
> For in Israel it is also written,
> "Prophecy is too great a thing for Baruch."

In Part II of "Baruch," Simpson goes over the ground again of the conflict between logos/longing and this world, showing how the conflict can influence a woman's life. Cousin Deborah had read too much. Literature was her ghostly lover and she was engaged to Pushkin. What chance did a man have competing with that?

> *On her wedding day she wept,*
> *and at night when they locked her in*
> *she kicked and beat on the door.*
> *She screamed. So much for the wedding!*
> *As soon as it was daylight, Brodsky—*
> *that was his name—drove back to Kiev*
> *like a man pursued, with his horses.*

What is left to say in Part III? Well, Simpson could talk about Americans. He does:

> *Even here in this rich country*
> *Scripture enters and sits down*
> *and lives with us like a relative.*
> *Taking the best chair in the house . . .*

He mentions that those who love literature often live among frayed carpets, walls with cracks in them. Then he restates the conflict again, brilliantly. This time we are on a train. Life on a train is banal. The wonderful banality of life that is so appealing, and makes such a genuine contrast to learning, is represented by a smoker car, with four or five men playing poker, happily, late at night. After the card playing, one of the men sits alone as he watches prairie lights, and the pale face from the unconscious appears, floating above the meadows and trees, reminding the man that love of the Torah is immortal. "He wishes to study the Torah." What has living in another country got to do with it? The love of learning never dies.

We notice there are no wild images. Every detail is tied into this stolid, hopelessly banal world, and yet these "flat" details make up a true and living mask for the face of the unconscious. The unconscious gives us its haunting look, which means, "Oh, God, are you going to be loyal to the Kaballa or to your family?" And we see that look. The eyes are alive, looking at us.

What can we say about that? I have to say terrific. In art, I want to see the "unknown" looking at me. I have a great thirst for that. I drink it in Conrad, in Chekhov, in *The Sorrows of Young Werther*, in *Moby Dick*, in the poetry of Russell Edson, in some Persian poetry, in a hundred works of art and psychological speculation. I don't have time to think, "It's better than so and so and not as good as Pound." If a man or a woman in art slowly creates a face we do not expect, we know that if we look at it closely, we will see the face of the unknown looking back. The face of the unknown is capable of many expressions—some so ecstatic we close our eyes, others that make the chest thump, as when an ant looks at us; and I am learning to judge poetry by how many looks like that I get in a book. If I get one or two, I am grateful and keep the book near me.

My words are a clumsy description of Louis Simpson's venture in his poetry. The advantages are clear: the poem is rooted well in this world, and by leaving the image, it adapts itself to the narrative; by leaving the private realm, it opens itself to other characters besides the poet.

What are the disadvantages of it? Most of us are asleep, having absorbed some sleepiness from tables and chairs and stoplights. By sticking to homey details, the writer is liable to describe people who are asleep. Second, objects get oppressive. When the poet concentrates on banal objects and details, these seem to get larger and larger and put us into despair. It seems as if things could not be otherwise than they are. Louis Simpson apparently has thought about this. I'll quote his poem about Hannibal:

> At times I am visited by a donkey
> who was once the great soldier Hannibal.
>
> The reason he didn't take Rome,
> he says, was a fear of success.
>
> Now that he has been psychoanalyzed
> he would, he is confident, rise to the occasion.
>
> But then he wouldn't be Hannibal.
> People would say, "It's a donkey."
>
> So, once more, Hannibal has decided . . .
> Moreover, if he succeeded, it wouldn't be Rome.

The conclusion of the poem seems to be that the substructure of events is impenetrable to the unconscious or conscious will. If Hannibal had not turned back, he wouldn't be Hannibal. When any writer makes a brave attempt to give the hard objects of the world attention, he may give them too much attention, and the inner transformative energies may be lost sight of. We would then experience the poem as circular and suffocating, in much the same way daily life is experienced as circular and suffocating. It is a risk. Louis Simpson takes it.

In many many poems he wins. For example, "The

Stevenson Poster," "The Middleaged Man," "The Sanc-
tuaries," and "The Tree Seat" are rich and brilliant. They
have the fragrance of the unknown in them, achieved
by means of this difficult and unusual discipline.

1958, 1960, 1976

James Dickey:

Imaginative Power and

Imaginative Collapse

BEASTS AND ANGELS

The poems of James Dickey describe a spiritual struggle.
We ordinarily think of this as the struggle of a man to
become an angel, but in Dickey's poems it seems more
like the struggle of an animal to become a man. The
being in the poem comes near some sudden transfor-
mation. As a Dickey poem begins, we see a man sleeping in the suburbs dreaming he is a deer; it is possible
this sleeper may be a deer dreaming it is a man.

His first book, *Into the Stone (1960)*, has a section called
Death. In many of his poems ears are listening for the
stirrings of the dead—the poet wonders if the dead are
turning over now, or walking about their houses. This
listening reminds us of the South, more than the Middle
West or New England. In a poem called "Listening to
Fox Hounds," Mr. Dickey is sitting with some other

hunters waiting for the hounds to call, signaling a scent. When Dickey sees how the face of the hound's owner lights up when the hound calls, he thinks that the man must have heard

> A thing like his own dead
> Speak out in a marvellous, helpless voice
> That he has been straining to hear.

In a poem called "Nimblewill," about hunting for Civil War relics with a mine detector, he is conscious of the dead there under the ground.

> For the dead have waited here
> A hundred years to create
> Only the look on the face
> Of my one brother.

In "The Sprinter's Sleep" we are given an entire scene after death. Six sprinters, all dead, are lined up on a track in the moonlight, "shaking out the muscles of their legs" "beginning to warm up" "among the shades." They dance each in their lane "where the glimmering tape is stretched across the end." We immediately notice one characteristic of Mr. Dickey's imagination: it seems to flower when he moves among the dead.

In his first book, Mr. Dickey tells us of the death of an uncle when the poet was a boy. It was a difficult death. "More kinship and majesty could not be." The boy carried the dead face away from the room, "down the dark stair as it became the whole of my mind," across the gravel of the driveway. At the end of the poem the poet questions whether it might not have been *he* who had the cancer and is now Death. We get the impression that this experience took from him some of his life certainty—his assurance that he is really alive.

In a number of poems, Mr. Dickey refers to an older brother who died of typhoid before the poet was born. When the poet dies, he wants to dress "in the gold of my waiting brother" who will bless him as he walks into heaven. Once more we have the sense that the poet feels the dead person is more alive than he is. He declares he was conceived only to replace that dead son. In "The Tree House," he maintains that this dead brother still guides the lives of himself and his younger brother.

> *Each nail in the house is now steadied*
> *By my dead brother's huge, freckled hand.*

The poet doubts whether he is alive at all. Yet when this doubt is strongest, he feels the sweet sensation he calls "moving at the heart of the world."

> *My green, graceful bones fill the air*
> *With sleeping birds. Alone, alone*
> *And with them I move gently.*
> *I move at the heart of the world.*

Again and again in the poems there is a feeling of being owned, and almost absorbed, by the dead. The poet is aware of this, and says speaking of his own son:

> *Before he came to life*
> *I was father to all the dead.*

This doubt that he really exists penetrates all the poems and leads to the idea of kingship. From believing himself nothing, he believes himself a king. This thought comes forward primarily in his second book, *Drowning with Others*, which Wesleyan published in 1962. Let us look at an odd poem called "The Scratch." The writer's wrist is scratched on a thorn in the woods, and a drop of blood appears. The first thought that occurs to him is that this drop of blood is a drop his sons will never inherit.

> *I have had no vision but this*
> *Of blood unable to pass*
> *Between father and son,*
> *Yet wedding the brain and the stone,*
> *The cock's cutting cry and the thorn,*
> *And binding me, whole, in a wood,*
> *To a prince of impossible blood.*
> *The rock shall inherit my soul.*
> *The gem at my wrist is dull*
> *And may or may never fall.*
> *Which will be, I do not know.*
> *I will dream of a crown till I do.*

What is the meaning of this crown? The long poem, "Dover: Believing in Kings" is all a "dream of a crown." It begins with a fairly straightforward account of the poet and his wife coming off the channel ferry at Dover; they go up to the top of the cliff and sleep there in a cabin that night, during which the electricity fails. The weird obsession with kings now takes over the poem.

He wonders if he will be passed down through his unborn son, or lost. If he receives the *Crown*, he will live. Looking out of the window, the candle lit, he imagines a crown coming toward him out of the night. He realizes the crown must come from *within*. He leaves his body, dreaming of various initiations and hardships; finally he slays the murderer under the sea, rises with the tide, becomes a man, lifts his father to his back, picks a queen, and begets a son.

When he awakes in the morning, he is still a man in blue jeans. Yet he suggests that these spiritual adventures lie buried in the mind of every man who is about to have a son.

The crown appears again in "The Owl King," the longest poem in *Drowning with Others*. The crown has become the crown of a tree. There are three characters in "The Owl King": the father, a blind son who is lost, and an owl king. The blind son, who is an image of a possible sexual punishment carried from father to son, remains unborn, lost in the forest. The father wanders looking for him; the owl king hears the boy calling and finds him. The owl reports, "I rose like the moon from my branch." Lighting down near the boy, the owl lifts his claw and puts it in the hand of the blind child. Then he takes the boy with him to his branch.

Who is the Owl King? The King of the Owls helps the boy to see, to *live:* The King of the Owls is an occult teacher:

> *I learn from the master of sight*
> *What to do when the sun is dead,*
> *How to make the great darkness work*
> *As it wants of itself to work.*

The child, then, helped by the Owl King, is able to move "at the heart of the world":

> *I walk in consuming glory*
> *Past the snake, the fox, and the mouse:*
> *I see as the owl king sees,*
> *By going in deeper than darkness.*

The boy learns to see—he gets the blue eyes of the man, and then the gold eyes of the owl and of the king. He now can penetrate animals and understand them.

> *Our double throne shall grow*
> *Forever, until I see*
> *The self of every substance*
> *As it crouches, hidden and free.*
> *The owl's face runs with tears*
> *As I take him in my arms*
> *In the glow of original light*
> *Of Heaven.*

The father meanwhile goes on singing in the moonlight, in love with the sound of his own voice, singing like a dog. Finally the blind child leaves the owl to help his father, and the poem ends.

This poem is a wonderful narrative; it is as strange as a Grimm brothers' tale. It is a narrative of some hidden events of the psyche and also, incidentally, an explanation of the poetry we are reading. The poet is trying to tell the reader that the person who wrote the poems is not James Dickey, the U.S. citizen who votes, but that the poems were written by a blind child and an owl sitting up on a pine tree! This is a good idea.

Kingship, significantly, is often embodied in animals. Animals are everywhere in Dickey's poetry. The poet is hunting them, or watching them, or slipping into their bodies, as into a new set of clothes. The animals are not emblematic beings, who exemplify some aspect of their creator, as in old Christian bestiaries, but quite to the contrary exist as if aware of their own stage of evolution. They are animals living after Darwin.

A hammerhead shark drifts by a boat in which the poet is sitting: the two look at each other. The poet knows that "The shark's brutal form never changes," and yet he feels, as in a hallucination, "a creature of light" rise from the ocean. This creature of light is what the man would like to become when he has evolved further.

The animals are usually met on hunting trips. Just as the hunting trip is an adventure for the body, the poem in which the spirit slips off and enters the minds of animals is an adventure for the soul. The poems have the hasty, excitable air of adventures. The being of an animal is glimpsed as something tremendously fluid— "a warm heaviness" flows "out of their mouths like souls." The wild animal is imagined as caught up in "the madness of hunting"; his spirit is sensitive—almost elegant. He tries to speak but cannot. Mr. Dickey emphasizes again and again this "silenced tongue" and at times suggests that if an animal could speak, he might become a god.

The animals' joy is associated with their yearning to evolve and speak. He describes animals at night in Georgia watching some human beings inside a screen porch:

> *Small blindly singing things,*
> *Seeming to rejoice*
> *Perpetually, without effort.*

Without knowing why
Or how they do it.

Why not imagine then a heaven of animals? Mr.
Dickey does so.

THE HEAVEN OF ANIMALS

Here they are. The soft eyes open.
If they have lived in a wood
It is a wood.
If they have lived on plains
It is grass rolling
Under their feet forever.

Having no souls, they have come,
Anyway, beyond their knowing.
Their instincts wholly bloom
And they rise.
The soft eyes open.

To match them, the landscape flowers,
Outdoing, desperately
Outdoing what is required:
The richest wood,
The deepest field.

For some of these,
It could not be the place
It is, without blood.
These hunt, as they have done,
But with claws and teeth grown perfect,

More deadly than they can believe.
They stalk more silently,

And crouch on the limbs of trees,
And their descent
Upon the bright backs of their prey

May take years
In a sovereign floating of joy.
And those that are hunted
Know this as their life,
Their reward: to walk

Under such trees in full knowledge
Of what is in glory above them,
And to feel no fear,
But acceptance, compliance.
Fulfilling themselves without pain

At the cycle's center,
They tremble, they walk
Under the tree,
They fall, they are torn,
They rise, they walk again.

Once more, there is the possibility of being "at the cycle's center." Wild nature is of help to man, then, because it helps the human to achieve the journey "to the heart of the world." "The Salt Marsh" touches on this idea. The advantage of a salt marsh full of reeds is that it is all alike: you can't tell where you are. If, then, you do not become afraid, but instead give in, and bend with the reeds—

> *helping their wave*
> *Upon wave upon wave upon wave*
> *By not opposing . . .*

—then you yourself can be included in their motion:

> *Among fields without promise of harvest,*
> *In their marvellous, spiritual walking*
> *Everywhere, anywhere.*

The bending reeds, walking and staying still, become an emblem of a spiritual state in men.

> *Can it be that the wounds of beasts,*
> *The hurts they inherit no words for,*
> *Are like the mouths*
> *Of holy beings . . . ?*

These sudden passages from the bestial to the angelic, which underly many of Dickey's poems, are unique and daring in conception. Yet we sometimes feel an uneasiness when we become aware that the human battleground between the bestial and the angelic is missing. It is the same uneasiness we remember feeling when we first read that the southern man supposedly thinks of a woman either as a beast or an angel.

We notice also that the passage from the bestial to the angelic takes place without regard to *character*. A strange quality of the book is that there is no talk of character. The slow struggle to improve character is the traditional way of supporting the volatile spiritual transformations. Without it, there is always the possibility the angelic world will fall back to the animal once more, again bypassing the human.

James Dickey embodies more of the South in his poems than any southern poet ever has. Not only does his content remind us of the South, but the style seems southern: it is quite plainly rhetoric, and a ghastly rhetoric is the worst weakness in these poems. At times the poems are like a compliment delivered to a southern belle before the Civil War—the phrases begin to unfold, led on one by the other, in a way at once highly organized and totally confused, and go on and on—the speech never seems to end.

Rhetoric exists here in a twisting of rhythm and language. The lines are forced, whether they like it or not, into a dactyllic rhythm—a heavy beat followed by two light ones. The opening of "Sleeping out at Easter," even though the short sentences seem simple, is really highly rhetorical.

> *All dark is now no more.*
> *This forest is drawing a light.*
> *All Presences change into trees.*
> *One eye opens slowly without me.*
> *My sight is the same as the sun's.*

Dickey's dactyllic power-mad rhythm often twists the arms of phrases that are unfortunate enough to fall into its hands: in "The Tree House" he says, "the half moon completely is shining"; the branches "Are full of small birds at their roundest." Terrible! Awful!

> *Occasionally, something weightless*
> *Touches the screen*
> *With its body, dies,*
> *Or is unmurmuringly hurt.*

One bird uncontrollably cries

Or though hand-shieldedly twice

Your spine tingles crystally, like salt

Awful! Awful! This is cruelty to adverbs. It ought to be a hanging offense. The dactyllic rhythm becomes monotonous, imposing phrases with a repetitive pattern: "That move with the moves of the spirit" or "Containing the sound I have made."

There is a curious narcissism in the poems. Henry Taylor, in his wild parody of Mr. Dickey, makes the poet talk of himself as an astronaut about to be rocketed up, who keeps speaking of "my body," "my tower," and the earth as "my green earth." Even though the rocket never took off, the astronaut reports at last, "I give three green cheers for myself." There is something to this criticism. Dickey's imagination is in the poem, but somehow, he contrives to get his ego-body in too. Often we feel surrounded in the poem by a kind of cloudy body substance, a kind of poetic musculature. In his constant references to his body, his fingers, his lungs, he simply gets in the way and blocks off the view. His body tends to push other people out of the poem— the personalities of others become fragmented. And the poems are too long. A poem begins, the rhetorical machine starts, and then dead matter is pulled into the poem to keep it going. Someone said that what is so wonderful about Mr. Dickey's poems is that miracles happen in them; the trouble is that the poem continues to go on after the miracle is over.

We have spoken of the faults in Mr. Dickey's poems. No matter how obvious they seem they cannot hide great originality. His work strikes us as original in current American poetry first of all because it is the exact opposite of the fashionable "my healthy limitations" school. Nemerov especially is a genius at these modest confessions of ordinariness. Other poets of the forties, like Ciardi, Nims, Whittemore, and Shapiro also pushed this "regular guy" poem to the forefront; it says essentially this: "I have healthy limitations; I have prudence; I'm very sane. I can't understand St. Theresa; as for beauty and nature, I can take it or leave it; it's wonderful to be so human!" This attitude has hardly enough spirit to sustain a filing clerk through life. It is ludicrous to see it adopted by poets. Mr. Dickey's originality, then, is that he discards this whole mediocre charade. He drives for something infinite in his poems. He exults, rants, says things he can't wholly understand, tries to imagine himself as a boundary-less person, like an animal or a god. He is aware that his "light body / Falls through the still years of [his] life / On great other wings than its own." He ignores everything that is ordinary and average; and tries in many poems to push to the very edge of his perceptions.

James Dickey has also found a way out of the old sterile war poem. The American war poems, à la Randall Jarrell, are almost always the same: the sensitive quirky lovable private contrasted to the nasty illiberal machine-tooled machine. Dickey discards all that. In Dickey's war, the machines are lovable and faithful, and the men either cruel or living hypnotized with a kind of numb animallike heroism. Imagination is actually nourished in the poem; the poet does not protest that war is no time for the imagination. Still the war is there, even the superstitious trancelike quality of war. Moreover, the poet is not a spectator, but a doer. Dickey, who was a fighter pilot in both World War II and the Korean War, a first-rate pilot, an ace in World War II, actually describes himself taking off in these fighter planes, "the matched, priceless engines around me." Here again he violates the conventional idea of the poet as an incompetent boob.

I have said all I understand about Dickey now, so I have to stop. When his imagination is interested, he carries tremendous physical energy into his poems. His courage is so great he does not fill the poem with phony Greek heroes as disguises, but instead places himself in the front of the poem, under clear glass, where you can see him for bad or good, and judge him as a fanatic, an animal killer, a lecher, a failure, or whatever you wish to. In his best poems something subterranean and preconscious is always present. He is like a big moose adapted somehow to living beneath the water in some calm inland lake. The moose is constantly rising to the surface and breaking water so he can see his own huge horns in the sunlight, and giving a fixed and strange smile to the frightened bourgeoisie out fishing.

1965

II
THE COLLAPSE OF JAMES DICKEY

Buckdancer's Choice has received a lot of attention from reviewers, but curiously no one has talked about the content. I thought the content of the book repulsive. The subject of the poems is power, and the tone of the book is gloating—a gloating about power over others.

"Slave Quarters" is a perfect example. A true work of art is sometimes able to be a kind of atonement. It moves into deep and painful regions of the memory, to areas most people cannot visit without wincing, and so do not visit. No one needs works of art like that more than we do. All over the American brain, there are huge areas like cutover forests, lobes made sterile by collective cruelty toward a race, by one egotistical murder after the other to keep a people in poverty as one keeps cows ... the psyche, faced with twentieth-century ideals, goes groggy with guilt. An art work can pierce that mass of guilts, gradually loosen it, help it to fall apart. But to do this, the work of art must carry real grief; it has to carry a masculine and adult sorrow. That is what Turgenev's, Chekhov's, and Tolstoy's work expressed when they talked about Russian serfdom. They told the truth both about the masters and about the serfs. Mr. Dickey's poem, "Slave Quarters," however, brings with it no grief: it gives the old romantic lying picture of the slaves and of the slaveowner. It is pure kitch, a *Saturday Evening Post* cover, retouched by the Marquis de Sade. Being sentimental, it does not help cure illness, but instead increases the illness. Far from expressing remorse, the poem conveys a childish longing for ultimate power, a desire to go back and simply commit the offences over again:

> *I look across low walls*
> *Of slave quarters, and feel my imagining loins*
> *Tense with the madness of owners*
> *To take off the Master's white clothes*
> *And slide all the way into moonlight*
> *Two hundred years old with this moon.*

The poet feels that the old South treated the Negro pretty much all right. He accepts, in fact, all the southern prejudices and, by adding artistic decoration to them, tries to make them charming. "Slave Quarters" pretends to be a poem about the moral issue of ownership, but instead lingers in the fantasies of ownership.

> *A child who belongs in no world   my hair in that boy*
> *Turned black   my skin*
> *Darkened by half   his, lightened*
> *By that half exactly   the beasts of Africa reduced*
> *To cave shadows flickering on his brow.*

The poem becomes ugly as he sniffs the Negro women, and prepares to do his great deed in the slave huts. He feels the same thrill from his power over dogs as over people:

> *In the yard where my dogs would smell*
> *For once what I totally am*
> *Flaming up in their brains as the*
> *   Master*

On the whole, I consider this poem one of the most repulsive poems in American literature. The tone is not of race prejudice, but of some incredible smugness be-yond race prejudice, a serene conviction that Negroes are objects. It is not great life-enhancing poetry as the critics burbled, but bad tasteless slurping verse. The language is dead and without feeling.

> *   and above*
> *A gull also crabs slowly,*

> *Tacks, jibes then turning the corner*
> *Of wind, receives himself like a brother*
> *As he glides down upon his reflection:*

The language after all can be no better than the quality
of the imagination, which in this poem is paralytic. The
poet is sure the Negro women would have welcomed
his rape, and when he envisions his half-Negro son
grown up, the well-worn pictures pop up in the shoot-
ing gallery: a heavyweight champion, a waiter in "epau-
letted coats," a parking lot attendant, a construction
worker, and so forth.

At the end the poet asks, thinking of his bastard Negro son, What would it be like, not to "acknowledge"
a son, but to "own" him? This question is a gesture in
the direction of the northern liberals, showing he knows
it is wrong to own people. The only *feeling* in the line
however is curiosity.

The tone of "Firebombing" is like the tone of "Slave
Quarters." As objects of sadism, the Negro women have
been replaced by the civilian population of Asia. We
shudder when we realize we are talking about the psyche of the United States. In these matters, Dickey balances on his shoulders an absolutely middle-class head.
He embraces the psychoses of the country and asks us
to wait until he dresses them up a bit with breathless
words: then all the liberals will see those psychoses are
really "life-giving."

"Firebombing" makes no real criticism of the American habit of firebombing Asians. It starts off with some
criticism of the pilot. We learn that the bomber pilot,
twenty years after his fire raids on the Japanese, feels
no remorse in his overstuffed kitchen, feels no guilt for

having burned people to death, feels no anguish, feels nothing, and this is intended as a complaint. He has burned up families:

> The others try to feel
> For them. Some can, it is often said.

The poem soon drops this complaint, however, and concentrates on the excitement of reliving the bombing.

> All leases of dogs
> Break under the first bombs, around those
> In bed, or late in the public baths: around those
> Who inch forward on their hands
> Into medicinal waters.

We notice the same curious obsession with power over dogs and over cows:

> Singing and twisting
> All the handles in heaven kicking
> The small cattle off their feet
> In a red costly blast

and people:

> With fire of mine like a cat
> Holding onto another man's walls

Everything, dogs, cats, cows, people, are objects to use power on. If this were a poem scarifying the American conscience for the napalm raids, we would feel differently. But this poem has no real anguish. If the anguish were real, we would feel terrible remorse as we read, we would stop what we were doing, we would break the television set with an ax, we would throw ourselves on the ground sobbing. We feel no such thing. The poem emphasizes the picturesque quality of firebombing instead, the lordly and attractive isolation of the pilot, the spectacular colors unfolding beneath, the way the fire spreads. It reminds one of Count Ciano's lyrical descriptions of his bombs falling on the Ethiopians in 1938: "The bombs opened beneath like great red flowers, beautiful in the center, like roses." Mr. Dickey remarks that in the cockpit he is "deep in aesthetic contemplation." "He sails artistically over / The resort towns." Some kind of hideous indifference numbs us, after having already numbed the language:

> *The heads come up with a roar*
> *Of Chicago fire:*

How cozy the whole thing seems to him is shown by:

> *Dogs trembling beneath me for hundreds of*
>   *miles, on many*
> *Islands, sleep-smelling that ungodly mixture*
> *Of napalm and high-octane fuel,*
> *Good bourbon and GI juice.*

The poet feels so little anguish, he provides charming little puns:

> *Where (my) lawn mower rests on its laurels.*

In its easy acceptance of brutality, the poem is deeply middle class. Dickey appears to be embarrassing the military establishment for its Japanese air raids, but he is actually performing a function for the establishment. He is teaching us that our way of dealing with military brutality is right: do it, later talk about it, and take two teaspoonfuls of remorse every seventh year. In short, if we read this poem right, we can go on living with napalm.

The third ugly poem is "The Fiend." "The Fiend" is a foggy, overwritten fantasy about another sort of power—this time the power the man who is utterly cold has over those who still feel human warmth and enthusiasm. It is about the power the Snow Queen has over the human children. The power is symbolized this time by a window peeper, who is sexually not quite all there. The poem begins with some good descriptions of window peeping, interiors of houses seen by a tree climber. The poem then tries to become "poetic" and talks about things Dickey used to make poetry out of—how the man interacts with the tree, how the tree itself perhaps is human too. The poem finally returns to its sadistic business at hand, the cold, excitable window peeper and the curious malignance he feels toward defenseless people, toward stenographers and working girls:

> and when she comes and takes down
> Her pants, he will casually follow her in
> like a door-to-door salesman
> The godlike movement of trees stiffening
> with him the light
> Of a hundred favored windows gone wrong

> somewhere in his glasses
> Where his knocked-off Panama hat was in
> his painfully vanishing hair.

The question is: why does the poem abruptly end there? My guess is that when the peeper went into the house, he cut the girl up with a knife. The knife is mentioned early in the poem. Of course speculations about what doesn't happen in a work of art are futile, like asking what Fortinbras did after Hamlet's death, but here the abrupt end calls for some explanation, and an escalation of sadism seems the only possibility. We realize reading it that something sadistic has entered wholeheartedly into Dickey's fantasy. The poem breaks off where it did, in my opinion, because Mr. Dickey realized that if he described the next scene he would lose his *New Yorker* audience. He didn't quite have the courage of his own sadism.

"Slave Quarters," "Firebombing," and "The Fiend," the three long pieces in the book, have a similar content and fail artistically for the same reasons. The language is inflated, the rhythms manufactured. All three are obsessed with power and driven by a childish longing for it, disguised only by the feeblest verbal veil. The humanistic mumblings at beginning or end hide the naked longing for power about as well as a Johnson white paper on foreign policy hides its own realities. The amazing thing is that none of the reviewers noticed what the poems were saying. Even reviewers as acute as David Ignatow, and as aware of American ambiguities, praised the pointless violence of these poems and accepted the poems' explanations of themselves at face value.

We can only lay this blindness to one thing: a brainwashing of readers by the New Critics. Their academic jabber about "personae" has taken root. Instead of thinking about the content, they instantly say, "Oh, that isn't Dickey in the 'Firebombing' poem! That is a persona!" This is supposed to solve everything. Yeats did use personae at times, a beggar, for example: yet as we read his beggar poems we are very conscious that Yeats is *not* the beggar. A great impersonal poem could be written on the old South and its slaves, shaped like "Slave Quarters." One could imagine an artist like Yeats in fact creating such a poem, yet all through the poem, we would be conscious that the poet was none of the characters, that he was outside of or beside the poem, his judgments made even more clear by their absence in the poem. But in "Slave Quarters" the umbilical cord has not been cut. Mr. Dickey is not standing outside the poem. On the contrary, the major characteristic of all these poems is their psychic blurriness. There are no personae. The New Critical ideas do not apply at all. Readers go on applying them anyway, in fear of the content they might have to face if they faced the poem as they face a human being.

Not all the poems in the book are as bad as these three, although all are touched by the same inflation. The best poem I think is "Sled Burial." "The Escape," about buying a grave lot, is also touching. Reading these two poems, some of the old affection I have always felt for Dickey's good poems returns. But even in the poems that are not sadistic, even in the "innocent" poems, a curious alienation takes place. James Dickey reminds you of some nineteenth-century flying enthusiast, whose deflated balloon is on the ground, and he is trying with tremendous wild power and large lungs to blow it up himself. In "The Shark's Parlor," he succeeds. As he puffs, the genial poem grows larger and larger. But then an unexpected thing happens: the balloon leaves without him. The poem floats away, we and the poet are left behind, standing in the same place we were before all the effort started. Fundamentally, "Shark's Parlor" has no meaning. Rilke thought that when the poem had meaning, it carried the author to a new place. Frost, too, said that a true poem, like a piece of ice on a hot stove, moves on the stream of its own melting, and by its end, the true poem is far away from its starting place. Thinking of Dickey's poems in this way, it is clear they are worked up. As someone said recently, Mr. Dickey takes his life and laminates poetry onto it.

When Mr. Dickey visits college campuses for readings, he makes clear his wholehearted support of the Vietnam War. This is his business, but we must note again the unity of the man and his work. Of course the pilot he describes feels no remorse. If the pilot he describes felt any remorse for the earlier firebombings, he would be against the firebombings now. As a poet and as a man, Mr. Dickey's attitudes are indistinguishable from standard middle-class attitudes. In an article about him, Mr. Dickey boasted that he had made $25,000 on poetry last year. Obviously his decision to make poetry a "career" like professional football or advertising is associated with the abrupt decline in the quality of his work. In any event, his decline from "A Mountain Tent" in *Drowning with Others* to "Slave Quarters" is catastrophic, enough to make you weep. One cannot help but feel that his depressing collapse represents some obscure defeat for the United States also. He began writing about 1950, writing honest criticism and sensitive poetry, and suddenly at the age of forty-three, we have a huge blubbery poet, pulling out southern language in long strings, like taffy, a toady to the government, supporting all movements toward Empire, a sort of Georgia cracker Kipling. Numerous American artists have collapsed over a period of years—John Dos Passos is an example—but in Dickey's case the process seems accelerated, as in a nightmare, or a movie someone is running too fast.

1967

Galway Kinnell:

The Hero

and the Old Farmer

I

Galway Kinnell admires in his poems the movement down into earthly body, dirt, appetite, gross desire, death, flies.

> *The fly*
> *I've just brushed*
> *from my face keeps buzzing*
> *about me, flesh-*
> *eater*
> *starved for the soul.*
> *One day I may learn to suffer*
> *his mizzling, sporadic stroll over eyelid and cheek,*
> *even be glad of his burnt singing . . .*
> *And we say our last goodbye*
> *to the fly last,*
> *the flesh-fly last,*

the absolute last,
the naked dirty reality of him last.

Kinnell resists a spirituality that urges us to lift too quickly away from the flesh, and he warns against "fulfillment" before the heavy work of incarnation has been done, knowing that the upward movement may result in bloodless purity and narcissistic obsession. Thoreau, referred to mockingly in Kinnell's "The Last River," exemplifies the dangers in bloodless purity:

> *a man of noble face*
> *sits on the iron bunk, wiping*
> *a pile of knifeblades clean*
> *in the rags of his body.*
> *My old hero. Should I be surprised? . . .*
>
> *Seeking love . . . love*
> *without human blood in it,*
> *that leaps above*
> *men and women, flesh and erections,*
> *which I thought I had found*
> *in a Massachusetts gravel bank one spring . . .*
> *seeking love . . .*
> *failing to know I loved most*
> *my purity . . .*

But a transcendent power does exist. When a lucky moment arrives, light shines from inside matter.

> *When the fallen apple rolls*
> *into the grass, the apple worm*
> *stops, then goes*

> *all the way through and looks out*
> *at the creation unopposed, the world*
> *made entirely of lovers.*

In fallen apples and fallen nature there remains something eternal and shining. To "go through" is to inhabit the world "made entirely of lovers": "And now everything changes. Look: / Ahead of us the meantimes is overflowing." Kinnell will not use angels as a metaphor for the streaming; instead he chooses milk bottles, or bees, or a moment by an ordinary wood fire.

> *On the path,*
> *by this wet site*
> *of old fires—*
> *black ashes, black stones, where tramps*
> *must have squatted down,*
> *gnawing on stream water,*
> *unhouseling themselves on cursed bread,*
> *failing to get warm at a twigfire—*
>
> *I stop,*
> *gather wet wood,*
> *cut dry shavings, and for her,*
> *whose face*
> *I held in my hands*
> *a few hours, whom I have back*
> *only to keep holding the space where she was,*
>
> *I light*
> *a small fire in the rain.*
>
> ("Under the Maud Moon")

A critic might apply biographical detail to explain this passage, but such explanation is beside the point. The

honoring of the transfigurative is present, and Kinnell
suggests that it is feminine in tone.

What is the proper route then to take toward this
"world made entirely by lovers"? As I understand it,
Kinnell says the fly or the porcupine may be more helpful than the angel. His suspicion of the transcendent,
or the falsely or too easily transcendent, invigorates each
step he takes. He prefers the porcupine route, no matter
how many blows to the snout he receives, rather than
take the path to heaven through purity. He is not put
off by porcupine behavior in human beings:

> *In character*
> *he resembles us in seven ways:*
> *he puts his mark on outhouses,*
> *he alchemizes by moonlight,*
> *he shits on the run,*
> *he uses his tail for climbing,*
> *he chuckles softly to himself when scared,*
> *he's overcrowded if there's more than one of him*
> > *per five acres,*
> *his eyes have their own inner redness.*

Ascension is not for the porcupine or the starfish. Kinnell insists on water, mud, and descent.

DAYBREAK

> *On the tidal mud, just before*
> > *sunset,*
> *dozens of starfishes*
> *were creeping. It was*
> *as though the mud were a sky*

and enormous, imperfect stars
moved across it as slowly
as the actual stars cross heaven.
All at once they stopped,
and as if they had simply
increased their receptivity
to gravity they sank down
into the mud; they faded down
into it and lay still; and by the time
pink of sunset broke across them
they were as invisible
as the true stars at daybreak.

In this masterpiece, Kinnell describes the process of sinking with utter clarity. One simply sinks down into matter; there is no apparent effort. When one sinks in the psyche, one does not lose touch with the world above earth. On the contrary the starfish resemble—in a way the physical eyes cannot see—"the true stars at daybreak." The aim then is to sink in such a way as to retain contact with the stars.

II

I am interested in an ancient earthlike personality in Kinnell who controls the poems from below. This earth-like personality, who reminds me of a farmer from 2000 B.C., lives by being attached. This farmer-personality is attached to Mother, to milk, to fireplace, to children in the father's arms, to pigs in a sack, to bears hibernating, to animals being hunted, to bears licking their young. Whatever the old farmer loves, Kinnell's imagination prefers. Kinnell's imagination, therefore, dwells on blackberries, sows, wet wood, frog ponds. The ancient obsessive, matter-loving being in him remains around matter, loves matter, holds to matter, and persists in his love. That farmer resembles the huge log he describes that rolls up the Oregon beach and down into the water over and over again, is once more tossed up, plunges down and submerges. The log knows only matter. This earthlike, loglike personality is insistent. Although not imaginative by its nature, it controls the imagination. Whatever the earthlike being dwells on, the sophisticated imagination will dwell on.

We are talking of contraries here. "Without contraries is no progression," Blake says. What is the other pole, then, to this earthlike being? It is the son-hero, the one who in the mother's womb received some intimation of a perfect union, of some sort of streaming that happens only or mostly in the bodiless spheres.

> *I want to lie out*
> *on my back under the thousand stars and think*
> *my way up among them, through them,*
> *and a little distance past them, and attain*
> *a moment of nearly absolute ignorance,*
> *if I can, if human mentality lets us.*
>
> ("The Seekonk Woods")

"I would be ignorant as the dawn," Yeats said. That son-hero hovers observant, witnessing, aware of incompleteness and completeness, of moments when a shining "heavens the earth," of moments of bodiless love, an intense union of two souls, transfiguration.

The son-hero is aware of the moments when the past

overlaps the future, and aware of the streaming that sometimes comes through.

> *Then I will go back*
> *to that silent evening, when the past just managed*
> *to overlap the future, if just by a trace, and the light*
> *that lives inside the eclipse doubles and shines*
> *through darkness the sparkling that heavens the*
>   *earth.*

("That Silent Evening")

The son-hero is young and light.

I now look on Galway Kinnell's poems not as speech created by an integrated personality, but as a conversation between the son-hero and the obsessive earth being. I think every man has experienced a similar split, and we don't know what to do about the dance that needs to go on between the two personalities. We don't get any instruction. The relationship between the old farmer and the son-hero changes as we get older.

With the most wonderful faithfulness, Galway Kinnell sustains the tension between these two. For Galway Kinnell is neither one. He is the one who remains alive and alert to the tension between them.

1987

Donald Hall:
Doing What You Want
to Do

I'm going to concentrate here on *The Happy Man*, more particularly on the long poem called "Shrubs Burnt Away," with sideways looks at other poems. In *The Happy Man* and his 1978 book called *Kicking the Leaves* Donald Hall is doing his most substantive work. Literarily, he has created a lively short line and a lively long line. He has overcome a tendency toward mechanical rhythm that his long line exhibited in the sixties and seventies. His short line, as apparent in the poem called "Whip-poor-will," is now positively elegant in its use of sound, and its pitch variations remind us of some of the best poems of William Carlos Williams.

One could also mention a spiritual advance. First of all, he works in *The Happy Man* to create an eye that can see granite as a form of grass; and he pulls heavy objects sometimes into the world of transparency and spirit. Several poems express the soul's longing to know other worlds.

> *Here love builds*
> *its mortal house, where today's wind carries*
> *a double scent of heaven and cut hay.*

Finally, in this book, he is able—for example, in the poem "The Baseball Players"—to see moments of eternity clearly in the midst of muddled daily life.

Psychologically, the book is complicated. The psychology in his early books tends to be clear—too clear, with naked oppositions of country and city, conscious and unconscious, repression and expression that take place against a mess of lies hinted at in the background. Now he brings the messy background to the foreground.

He wrote in earlier books as a critic of his father's side of the family. The men on his father's side worked mainly as businessmen in the last two generations; on his mother's side there were farmers and, among both men and women, schoolteachers. Donald Hall's father gave up a possible career as a prep-school teacher to work in his own father's dairy in Hamden, Connecticut. All his life he chided himself, Donald Hall says, for not doing *what he wanted to do*. When Donald as a boy visited the New Hampshire farm owned by the mother's side of his family, he experienced the traditional life of the farmer and preferred that to the life in Hamden. Comparing the two ways, he criticized his father's way and, beyond that, all suburban life and, beyond that, the entire middle class. He praised in his poems and prose what he had learned to love in New Hampshire: the slow pace of farm life, the alternation of seasons, the ritual of haying, the care for cattle and other animals, the extended families, the relatedness. This life he described beautifully in *String Too Short to Be Saved,* a prose book that is still a masterpiece of recollection.

During the years he attacked the middle class most sharply, he made his living as a university professor. Such a vocation proved to be, in view of his psychology, a hard place in which to stand. It entangled him in self-shaming on the one hand, and an uneasy nostalgia for a vanished life on the other.

He brought the two sides closer together by moving into the old New Hampshire farmhouse in 1975, establishing his life with Jane Kenyon, each of them doing what they do. He is not a farmer; he doesn't farm the land, but he does live firmly on it.

Whether a person does what he or she wants to do becomes a prominent theme in "Shrubs Burnt Away," and we will turn to that poem now. The speakers in the poem do not have names, so one needs to read carefully to find out who is who. The lives evoked do not correspond in any detail to the lives of Donald Hall's father and mother, grandmother, and so forth, so the poem is not strictly autobiographical. The poem is *composed* and we have a right then to consider the chosen details important and intentional.

The main speaker is middle-aged, a drinker, a smoker, nostalgic, fond of his yellow chair, adulterous in the past, now Calvinist around sexuality, full of memories of his childhood, aware of betrayals he has himself done. He has a mother who he mentions sang songs to him when he was a child, and he refers briefly to his father, who worked in a lumberyard. We'll call the main speaker Horace, just for fun.

The second main speaker, who is a woman, has a great number of stories to tell. Her words are set in quotation marks so we can easily identify her talk. She is not related to the first speaker, and apparently the two have never even met each other. She loved drawing and painting when she was a young girl; then for a long time did not do "what she wanted to do." In later age she has become an active and well-known sculptor. We'll call her Henrietta, just to have a name for her.

Henrietta tells several stories about her own parents. Her mother was alcoholic, hooked on pills, and an adulteress as well. Henrietta as a child was looking for a playmate named Bingo.

> *"We were chasing each other and ran into a clearing*
> *And found Bingo and Harold's father and my mother*
> *Drunk, rolling on the grass with their clothes off."*

Henrietta's father, cuckolded in this way, throws a drink into her mother's face and then drives at high speeds down the dark roads. Apparently some time later he dies in a car crash.

Henrietta's reminiscences include some scenes that appear to be drawn from Donald Hall's childhood memories. The imagined family that lives the life that the poet has been so idealistic about shows a dark and murky history when investigated. That fact means to me that we don't have a simple contrast anymore—a bad suburb versus a good farm. The writer brings in daydreams and night dreams; and the people living on the "good farm" have disturbing dreams. Horace tells one dream of a sexual party, and Henrietta describes two dreams, one of a plane crash and one of the execution of children. Horace daydreams about floods carrying away houses, of middle-class homes being burned down, and so on. Both of the speakers appear to have been let down by the older generation in some way. Both have experienced early failures that seem to reflect long-standing family neuroses. Horace says,

I lay in the dark hearing trees scrape
like Hauptmann's ladder on the gray clapboard.
Downstairs the radio diminished, Bing Crosby,
and I heard voices like logs burning, flames
rising and falling, one high and steady, one
urgent and quick. If I cried, if I called . . . I called
softly, sore in the wrapped dark, but there was
*   nothing,*
I was nothing, the light's line at the closed door faint.
I called again; I heard her steps:—
Light swept in like a broom from the opening door

and my head lay warm on her shoulder, and her breath
sang in my ear—A Long Long Trail A-winding,
Backward Turn Backward O Time in Your Flight . . .
In the next room a drawer banged shut. When my
*   father*
lay dying at fifty-one, he could not deliver
the graduation speech at Putnam Avenue School
near the house he was born in. Taking my father's
place, my head shook like a plucked wire.
I told the fourteen-year-olds:
Never do anything except what you want to do . . .

Once a little boy and his sister—my mother lay
on top of the quilt, narrow and tense, whispering—
found boards piled up, deep in the woods, and nails,
and built a house for themselves, and nobody knew
that they built their house each day in the woods . . .

I listened and fell asleep, like a baby full of milk,
and carried their house into sleep where I built it
board by board all night, each night
from the beginning; from the pile of boards I built it,
painted it, put doorknobs on it . . .

In the song Hall is quoting, "Backward Turn Backward
O Time in Your Flight," the following line is "Make me
a child again just for tonight."

Is there any doubt that a longing for union with the
mother underlies many of these lines and hovers around
the stories of grown-ups told elsewhere in the poem?
We have a situation that the Freudians called the fundamental situation: longing for early union with the
mother, hostility toward the father—sometimes con-
veyed by condescension—and attraction to tales of sexual activity seen by children. The question being asked
is "Where does the sexual libido—unused—in the child
go?" Freudians traditionally fail to imagine any mythological place where this libido could go—for example,
toward "The Heavenly Pair," to the Imagined Woman,
to Aphrodite. This failure of imagination traps the child
in its constantly disappointed state. The woman to
whom all these incestuous longings go—the personal
mother—cannot produce the remembered Eden and so
disappoints the child. Everyone is disappointed. The
psyche as a result is not a good container: desire energy
leaks out in constant fantasy toward the personal
mother, and the psyche then as a result cannot maintain
its firm desire to achieve an artist's life. The inability to
"do what you want to do" is precisely the speaker's
charge against his own father and Henrietta's charge
against herself and against her mother.

There is much helplessness and victimization in the stories: children abandoned in the crib by the mother, mistreated, forced to see what they don't want to see. It's as if their lives were eaten up by older people. Henrietta recalls,

> "The year after my father burned in the wrecked car,
> My mother came home early from the job she hated
> teaching bookkeeping at the secretarial college.
> Sometimes she wept because she had flunked someone
> she had caught cheating. Each day I comforted her;
> I was fifteen years old. I cooked supper for her—
> hamburgers and hot dogs, baked beans, corn niblets.
> Once I took a recipe from Confidential Chat,
> using asparagus soup, Ritz crackers, and water
>   chestnuts.
> She said I would make some man happy."

The mood is psychic despair, depression, passivity. Neither the main speaker nor Henrietta are doing what they want to do and the older generation seems to have failed at that, too. The main speaker as a boy was doing what grown-ups do, for example, milking cows and calling calves. We don't see the boy playing the games of children his own age. Nostalgia may be associated with having grown-up playmates when young. We know from other poems that Donald Hall on the farm as a boy played the grown-up games with the grown-ups, but they are dead. Does that mean that when he plays he must play with the dead people? Well, that is the way it is.

Horace tells one of his dreams:

There was the dream of the party: a French farce,
frolic behind curtains, exits and entrances—
like a child fooling parents. I departed
alone on a bus that bumped down the white staircase
of the mansion over the bodies of three women
who stood complacent and pretty in the bus's way,
their faces familiar as photographs. When I looked
back from the bus's rear window at their bodies,
they waved to me although they were dead:—
They forgave me because no one was driving the bus.

The dream hints at some sort of depreciation of Eros.
A bus rolls over three women; they wave and they for-
give the dreamer "because no one was driving the bus."
Henrietta dreamed this scene:

"I wait for the plane inside a blockhouse
at the airport's edge; then the cement walls vibrate
as if an earthquake shook them. I understand at once:
The plane from Ireland has crashed trying to land.
Immediately I watch a conveyor belt
remove bodies covered with brown army blankets
from the broken snake of the fuselage. One of the dead
sits up abruptly, points a finger at me,
and stares accusingly. It is an old man with an erection;
then I notice that all of the dead are men."

This dream might imply that the young male Eros has
crashed or died—that is "the plane from Ireland"—
while the only Eros left is associated with old men.
   All through the poem we notice a loss of energy
through alcohol and aimlessness. Mythologically I sense
some sort of being or figure who eats the forward en-

ergy, particularly of the men. Toward the end of "Shrubs Burnt Away," one last dream of Henrietta is recounted; in it an ominous figure appears. It is a bee-keeper or a person with a beekeeper's masked face. This figure supervises the cutting up of the children.

> "I am sad in the convenient white kitchen, dreaming
> that I weep as I start making dinner.
> The children themselves weep, bringing their sentences
> on small folded squares of blue paper.
> They will take pills to die without disturbance.
> I help them count the pills out, and arrange
> pillows for their comfort as they become sleepy.
> While I slice onions and peppers on the breadboard,
> someone whose identity hovers just out of sight, the
>   way
> a beekeeper's mask darkens a face,
>
> "walks up the busy street and enters the kitchen
> to instruct me in butchering the children.
> The visitor picks up the long rag doll and with scissors
> carefully cuts the doll's limbs at the joints,
> teaching me expertly, with anatomical explanations
> and a scientific vocabulary, while cutting and
>   preparing
> the model, then places the doll's parts
> on a high shelf, arranged with the gaps of
>   dismemberment
> visible, so that I may consult it while cutting,
> as I must do, as it seems that I want to do."

The poem as a whole lays out a description, even a narrative, of the sort of life that activates the beekeeper.

I would say that this figure has moved in to grow enormous at the expense of the passive or the undifferentiated male soul. What can Henrietta or the main speaker do when they feel themselves threatened by this beekeeper? Elsewhere in the book the writer offers an option—living a boring conventional life unobserved. The poem is called "Mr. Wakeville on Interstate 90":

> *"Now I will abandon the route of my life*
> *as my shadowy wives abandon me, taking my children.*
> *I will stop somewhere. I will park in a summer street*
> *where the days tick like metal in the stillness.*
> *I will rent the room over Bert's Modern Barbershop*
> *where the* TO LET *sign leans in the plateglass window;*
> *or I will buy the brown* BUNGALOW FOR SALE.
>
> *"I will work forty hours a week clerking at the*
>   *paintstore.*
> *On Fridays I will cash my paycheck at Six Rivers Bank*
> *and stop at Harvey's Market and talk with Harvey.*
> *Walking on Maple Street I will speak to everyone.*
> *At basketball games I will cheer for my neighbors'*
>   *sons.*
> *I will watch my neighbors' daughters grow up, marry,*
> *raise children. The joints of my fingers will stiffen.*
>
> *"There will be no room inside me for other places.*
> *I will attend funerals regularly and weddings.*
> *I will chat with the mailman when he comes on*
>   *Saturdays.*
> *I will shake my head when I hear of the florist*
> *who drops dead in the greenhouse over a flat of*
>   *pansies;*
> *I spoke with her only yesterday . . .*

*When lawyer elopes with babysitter I will shake my
   head.*

*"When Harvey's boy enlists in the Navy
I will wave goodbye at the Trailways Depot with the
   others.
I will vote Democratic; I will vote Republican.
I will applaud the valedictorian at graduation
and wish her well as she goes away to the university
and weep as she goes away. I will live in a steady joy;
I will exult in the ecstasy of my concealment."*

Only tremendous fear could force a man to contemplate
such a boring life. If he lives so, apparently he will
escape the beekeeper's notice; or alternately, he will
already have diminished himself so much that there is
no more to diminish. What else do we deserve? We were
conceived by the rabble left behind when the aristocrats
went to Ceylon.

*While Lady Ann grew pale playing the piano, and lay
       late in bed aging,
she regretted Rathwell who ran off to Ceylon with his
       indescribable
desires, and vanished—leaving her to the servants who
       poached, larked,
drank up the cellar, emigrated without notice, copulated,
       conceived, and begot us.*

(The Revolution)

We can say that Horace in the long poem is very hard
on himself. His critical "I" is overactive, sees no redeeming feature in the reckless living of sexual impulse,
and sees no redeeming feature even in old love affairs.

◆ 205 ◆

The world is a bed, I announce; my love agrees.
A hundred or a thousand times our eyes encounter;
each time the clothes slough off, anatomies
of slippery flesh connect again
on the world's bed, and the crescent of nerves
describes itself again in the wretched
generality of bliss. If we are each the same
on the world's bed, if we are each manikins of the other
then the multitude is one and one is the multitude;
many and one we perform procedures of comfort.

In several poems, the speaker longs to die—by car crash, or rifle. The beekeeper encourages the interior critic. I feel considerable art in this introduction of the beekeeper. Most people understand the beekeeper very well, and know how much damage he has caused their lives. He judges life, cuts it up, puts its possibilities to sleep, acts like the judge at an unfair trial. Of course, we have no right to say that the beekeeper is "he." The author carefully avoids pronouns. The poem about the old woman in the rocker who observes male suicides with equanimity suggests that the beekeeper may be female. Whether male or female in tone, the beekeeper assists in the cutting up on the dolls and the severing of life from its desire ground. I think we have to thank Donald Hall for going into this serious brooding as deeply as he has. He may be afraid, but he continues to work anyway.

I am not saying that Donald Hall intended to lay out these last observations about the beekeeper or the Old Lady in the Rocker who eats libido, particularly, it seems to me, libido when it has lost its goal, but that is what the poems say. I think that with his image of the beekeeper he has added an important contemporary detail to the ancient pictures of the Devourer, that is the Great Mother in her eating mood or the Great Father in his eating mood. The courage of the writer lies in his repeating: something or someone has eaten up my family, or more accurately, has eaten up the desire-energy of the two families being described. That is enough to say in one poem.

Understanding that expressed fear helps us to set an otherwise puzzling epigraph into place. If we imagine the Devourer as a tiger, we can understand the paragraph from Hsu Hsia-K'o: "Mi-t'o Temple after Thirty li. A most desolate spot. . . . For fear of them hiding tigers, all trees and shrubs have been burnt." The book's epigraph from Tolstoy goes

> *Behold me then, a man happy and in good health,*
> *hiding the rope in order not to hang myself to the*
> *rafters of the room where every night I went to*
> *sleep alone; behold me no longer shooting, lest*
> *I should yield to the too easy temptation . . .*

1989

The Mastery of
John Logan

I
SENSUALITY AND LUMINOSITY

John Logan is one of the five or six finest poets to emerge in the United States in the last decades. He has won a position of considerable respect without the help of the major schools or their magazines. Most of the Black Mountain poets were unable to swallow a poetry that takes the Christian God seriously; the academics are unable to swallow a poetry both Christian and bristly, which looks wild and matted to them, like the head of a desert fanatic.

In the title poem of *Spring of the Thief*, he remarks that perhaps "freshness is the changed name of God." "I bear him in the ocean of my blood / and in the pulp of my enormous head. / He lives beneath the unkempt potter's grass of my belly and chest. / I feel his terrible, aged heart / moving under mine. . . . "

We can feel in this quotation Logan's powerful phrasing—the words leave his hands bent permanently into their phrases and the phrases are curved so as to carry emotion better. He has a great gift for the phrase that carries deep emotion—and carries it somehow invisibly, in ways impossible to pin down. In his work, he shows himself again and again able to create a poem without the hectic surface that so many poets depend on to carry emotion. Instead he moves us simply by moving language.

> *The partridge has some sadness or other*
> *knocking softly in his throat as a missing motor . . .*

In "Spring of the Thief," Logan asks what is the new name, the winter name, of God—"where is his winter home?" He writes a poetry in which heavy, turgid sensuality, whirling like water in a ditch after a sudden rainstorm, is mingled with a luminous spiritual leaping and a desire that everything in the world shall shine from within.

II
HIS RANGE OF LANGUAGE

It's not clear to me why his poems are able to move us, when so many other poems fail. Surely the extraordinary range of language has something to do with it— the shifts in tone keep our feelings alive as we read. Speaking of a work glove that was stiffened with white paint:

> *It is the left glove, the hand of the Magus,*
> *of all who come late or by devious ways*
> *oblique to honor Christ.*

There the language is dignified and elaborate. In "The Thirty-Three Ring Circus," a linked collection of tiny poems, the language is swift and sure, and resembles the simple language of Neruda in his *Odas Elementales:*

> *The man who*
> *stands on one*
> *finger, on*
> *one edge of*
> *a ladder*
> *on one leg,*
> *on a ball,*
> *tentative*
> *as a soul.*

Throughout the poem, the language changes abruptly and masterfully, alternating formal and street tones:

> *An old, slop-hat, melancholy*
> *father, no Telemachus found,*
> *rushes weeping about the tent and ground.*

> *After the tent is down,*
> *the circus owner, having*
> *slept over, sets out*
> *in his red car, feeding*
> *his silver slug of a house*
> *over the waste he is lord of.*

One of Logan's poems I love the most is "Eight Poems on Portraits of the Foot" (after some close-up photographs of human feet that Aaron Siskind did). The yearning everything alive feels to change into something still more alive is brought forward:

> *It is the wish*
> *for some genuine change other than our death*
> *that lets us feel (with the fingers of mind)*
> *how much the foot desires to be a hand.*

The language in this poem does not change mood so much as speed. Logan lets it hurtle forward, then suddenly slows it down. These changes too keep our feelings alive.

> *The foot is more secret, more obscene,*
> *its beauty more difficultly won—*
> *is thick with skin and*
> *so is more ashamed than the hand.*
>
> *One nestled in the arched back of the other*
> *is like a lover*
> *trying to learn to love.*
>
> *A squid or a slug, hope still alive*
> *inside its mute flesh*
> *for the grace and speed of a fish.*
>
> *Sperm in the womb quickens to a man.*
> *The man yearns toward his poem.*

The language opens and closes like a heart valve in slow motion.

III
THE WIDE POLES OF THOUGHT

Reading in Logan's poems, one often stumbles on something totally unexpected: one finds a long poem on the old mechanist, La Mettrie; in the middle of a poem on Diogenes, De Rougemont turns up. His poem on the English romantic poets describes mainly Shelley's brain cooking on the Italian pyre and certain leeches over Byron's eye. References to his family are equally odd. We gather from the poems that Logan's mother died while the poet was still very young. There is a poem on the mother that suggests that the orphaned poet thought for many years in his early childhood that his mother was a red Irish dog. Metaphors are very strange when examined: he compares his long, ragged poems to children's sparklers; Heine's father to a tree of frost. He likes the widest poles of thought; before a poem, Logan quotes both these ideas: "The tongue fits to the teeth and the palate by Number, pouring forth letters and words" (St. Augustine); and "Years ago I came to the conclusion that poetry too is nothing but an oral outlet" (A. A. Brill, M.D.). This strangeness is interesting, but it is present in any good poetry.

In Logan an energy comes from within and results in honesty and a dislike of hokum. As Logan says of Rimbaud while a child:

> He travelled alone in his room
> Lying on a canvas piece
> Of sail harsh to skin . . .
> . . . he carved the table's
> Edge in the shape of a spinet:
> But couldn't stand the braid and
> Fat of the township band.

This energy comes from sources inaccessible to the man who possesses or surrounds the energy. He ex-

presses this much in the epigraph to the Rimbaud poem:
"So much the worse for the wood that finds it's a violin."
Rimbaud thought he saw this energy in Verlaine:

> He saw in Verlaine a child
> Of Sun—burnt by the ancient
> Memory, moved on the ancient
> Sunwarmed flank: struck
> As the great brass bells
> At the breasts of the cattle of the sun:
> Pierced or wheeled by the sun—
> Keen tips of the ancient horns.
> But Verlaine, stuck by an ordinary
> Arrow, moved with the faith
> Of his fathers and made a minor sound . . .

Of Rimbaud it was true: he did possess the energy.

> Some are moved as the gray
> Eyed Io by the god
> From home and call: are hurried
> To the drowsy lengths of the reed . . .
> Some have the face of a god,
> Some have the tooth of a swan, or the laughable
> Lust-sad eye of the calf.

The suggestion that such a man as Rimbaud has in
him a god, a swan, or a calf is evidently one of the
things he means by calling the poem "The *Lives* of the
Poet." Logan believes this intense kind of man to be
moved by several energies, several persons inside him:

> *The weight*
> *Of the gold about his waist*
> *Shall make him sick.*

He understands Rimbaud to be great because he is the possessor of the energy even against his will.

IV
HEINE AND THE MANY BEINGS INSIDE US

Let us look at the poem on Heine. The first stanza is a rich tissue of contradictions.

> *Heine's mother was a monster*
> *Who had him trained*
> *In business, war and law;*
> *In the first she failed the best:*
> *At work in his uncle's office*
> *He turned a book of Ovid's*
> *Into Yiddish. . . .*

These human contradictions in terms, such as the fourth line: "In the first she failed the best," evoke the fantastic confusion in human actions and feelings partially caused, according to Logan, by the multiplicity of beings inside everyone.

This abundant confusion inside Heine, a confusion also of wife and mother, is expressed again when Logan tells of Heine's leaving his wife at home in Paris, while he went into exile:

> *He left his mother I mean*
> *His other at home*

> With her nervous bird and her
> Shrieking tantrums—or else
> He left the bird with the wife,
> Et cetera . . .

Because of the existence of these many inward beings, the identity of men keeps shifting.

> . . . he wrote her a letter a
> Day like a scolding parent
> Afraid she'd become a Paris
> Whore as he hoped she would
> (And as he was) . . .

In the Heine poem, the indecision between mother and wife, so often present in the immature man, occurs on an heroic plane:

> He called his mother a dear old
> "Pussy cat";
> His wife was a "wild cat"; . . .

He himself is both son and father:

> As soon as he left himself
> To the needs of a wife
> He was shook to find in the face
> In the mirror the eyes of his father
> When his face had started to fade: . . .

In Heine, the great energy within often takes the opposite forms of Jew and Christian, or of son and husband. Heine was temporarily a Christian and tem-

porarily, also, a husband. Logan makes it clear that
Heine ultimately chooses to become the Jew and to become the son, rejecting the other two ("He never became
the husband"). The implied suggestion that to be a Jew
is like being an eternal son, and to be a Christian is like
being an eternal husband, is very interesting and leads
us toward new strange thoughts.

At any rate, as Heine grows older, he sinks back toward being a son:

> *He began to be blind, and gave in*
> *To a kind of paralysis that made him*
> *Lift the lid of his eye*
> *By hand to see his wife.*

To me, to be able to evoke the detail of Heine's having
to lift his own eyelid to see his wife, and to let that stand
as an image of the profound mysteries of a man sinking
back to sonhood, is brilliant. In lines like this, Logan
writes not so much with images as with *details*—yet
those details take on some power far beyond their own,
and seem to glow.

At other times, he uses images. An image, as I understand it, brings together different thoughts by inexplicable means. Logan writes of Heine's descent to
sonhood:

> *At the end, cones of opium,*
> *Burned on his spine, helped him*
> *To dream of a younger father*
> *Doing his hair in a snow of powder.*

In the next stanza Heine's father becomes a tremendous
white tree:

> *He tried to kiss his father's*
> *Hand but his pink*
>
> *Finger was stiff as sticks*
> *And suddenly all of him shifts—*
> *A glorious tree of frost!*
> *Unburdened of the sullied flesh.*

His death is described in this way:

> *His soft old flesh slipped*
> *Inside its great*
> *Trunk with a sound he held*
> *Too long inside his skull.*

That image is extremely intricate and bold at the same time. Just as the snow of powder gradually changed to the frosted tree, so the image of the tree trunk, slightly shifted, is still kept, and some silent and terrifying sound is evoked from it, the image suggesting also for the last time the multiple beings inside Heine.

Logan has written a fine poem on St. Catherine. He evokes her profusion of persons by comparing her to Joan of Arc, Christ, and Rimbaud. We remember that Logan used as an epigraph for one of his collections Melville's sentence "I am a frigate full of a thousand souls." In the poem on St. Catherine Logan suggests that some of the persons inside her were men. He suggests that part of the explanation of her power is hidden in the detail from her legend that "she is buried on old Moses' mountain."

> *I want to know in what way it is true*
> *That she is buried on old Moses' mountain,*

> *Her slender relics and the laws of women*
> *Mingling with the relics and the laws of men.*

Logan's first book was called *Cycle for Mother Cabrini*. In it there is a narrative poem called "A Short Life of the Hermit." Here the Christian mystic is discussed. The poem describes a typical Egyptian anchorite of the first centuries after Christ: "He sprung of highborn parents," but did not take to school. "In fact / Consistently despised / Your ancient learning." "He lacked a business sense." Logan writes already here with sarcasm, very different from the irony of the followers of Donne.

> *At first he saved a bit*
> *To meet a maiden sister's*
> *Need for funds, until*
> *Impatient at a Sunday text*
> *He took the sister to the nuns.*

At last the anchorite learns the "narrow wisdom of the bee," and after some temptations locks himself in a tomb. He stays there for twenty years, meeting many devils, who, as he later describes them, "hiss and prance," but, if not looked at, "seem to fall / Into a melancholy fit / Like an angry child." By his bare style Logan suggests this life of almost incredible nervous tension.

> *Once he made a basket*
> *Out of stems of reed*
> *And felt a gentle tugging*
> *In his hand; and met*
> *A giant with the withered*

Face of birds and long
And whitened arms of men,
Which at the secret name snapped
Into sticks of reed.

Those who go into the desert, of course, do not help society; their gifts are not what the world wants or would like to have.

This is the problem of an anchorite, and one reason there are so few of them today. Society today wants everyone to take part in the outer world, to pay taxes, and give it support. Most people act responsibly. John Logan supported his wife and nine children with regular teaching jobs and occasional extra jobs. He certainly gives society back as much as it gives him. It is interesting, then, that instead of defending his domestic position, as most poets do, he spends his energy understanding the opposite position—that of the anchorite! And he understands it better than any other American poet. The refusal to give anything to society is an old act, which Logan accepts with some amiability. He sums up the quality of the anchorite at the close of the poem in a single line:

He died
Old and left the skin of a goat.

V
THE GIFT OF LIGHT

We learn as we read Logan's poems to love a certain lucidity of light. In his poem on La Mettrie in his first book, the poet says he cannot agree with the mechanist:

> *For once there was*
> *A blurred and giddy light*
> *In my enormous eyes.*

Such a light occurs once more in a poem in *Ghosts of the Heart* called "Picnic":

> *It was then some bright thing came in my eyes,*
> *Starting at the back of them and flowing*
> *Suddenly through my head and down my arms . . .*
>
> *And Ruth played with shells she found in the creek,*
> *As I watched. Her small wrist which was so sweet*
> *To me turned by her breast and the shells dropped*
> *Green, white, blue, easily into her lap,*
> *Passing light through themselves. She gave the pale*
> *Shells to me, and got up and touched her lips*
> *With her light hands, and we walked down slowly*
> *To play the school games with the others.*

Logan's poems spring from what might be called an obscure experience of light.

VI
HIS LIVING, SWAYING LANGUAGE

I feel in Logan's poems always that the language is being used to build something, rather than to reflect something. We can imagine phrases as a series of wood chunks that the speaker can pile on top of each other, to build castles, or to reach apples high on a tree.

John Logan's language is always muscular and masculine, and he has always had a vision of language as something a man speaks to get off the earth, to cancel gravity temporarily. As he grows older, this element becomes stronger. No one alive has his fantastic power with adjectives. His sense for adjectives is really a love for the magnificence of the universe—there above us, which we can't quite reach. Here are his adjectives for a python in "The Zoo" from *Zigzag Walk*:

> The vicious, obvious and obscene
> greedy-eyed old python
> hauls itself along.

At times he builds slowly, laying down flight stairs upward, then, realizing what a hard time grandeur has on this planet, suddenly pulls it all down in a second:

> Look
> even the great brown handsome official Kodiac
> bear
> has caramel in its hair.
>
> Twenty charming little tropical monkey kids
> jabber in the phony trees. The gibbon is un-
>   kempt.
> The yellow baboons bark, and they travel in
>   groups.
> There, ugly and alone,
> awful and no longer young,
> is that ornery thing
> an orangutan.
> Disconsolate, contrite,
> red-haired widow who was once a wife

you pace and turn, and turn and pace
then sit on your repulsive ass
and with a hairy hand
and thumb delicately pinch an egg and
kiss its juice deep into your head.
Oh misery! Misery! You wretched bride.

John Logan braids language, making a whip that he hits himself with, or a jungle-vine rope with which he lets himself down dangerous cliffs. In his greatest poems he creates some sort of weaving, living, headed *thing*— all muscle, weaving about in the air, swaying. Its motions are curiously like the motions emotions make as they rise from the unconscious, and we feel strange because we know these motions: we have seen them at night since birth each time an emotion rises toward a dream; and as in a dream, we have no choice: we are moved. John Logan's creation of this living swaying poem out of American language is a discovery, a great triumph.

If a man visualizes language as if it were a block of wood, or a snake's body, that is, something with cubic space, he is not seeing it only from above, or below, but also from the side—he is walking *around* it.

John Logan is one of the very few masters of sound we now have. The Russians have, among others, Voznesensky. Voznesensky's poetry, like Logan's, is basically a poetry of the body. I think the reason Voznesensky's poems are so powerful in sound is because he is not exploiting sound in the head way—as Auden does sometimes—but because he is adapting the sounds to express body motions. His poems are rooted in the muscle system and in the chest system, as Neruda's sound is rooted in the stomach and intestinal system. A poem like Voznesensky's "Goya" is made of body movements—a woman's corpse swinging from a rope, a bell's tongue moving—these movements have found "embodiments," in the body of sound.

So also in John Logan's work we see sounds chosen by the body intelligence. He says of some Pacific rocks:

> *A little way above and to the left, the gull*
> *folks form*
> *quiet lines of their own.*
> *They wait along the brilliant height,*
> *and then, when its time,*
> *fling them-*
> *selves off into the wide*
> *arcs and dips of their angelic suicides.*

We can find these embodiments in language of body movements everywhere in his poems; his Hawaii poem is brilliant in this respect. He says of driftwood logs:

> *Here the logs lie like lovers*
> *short by long, benign,*
> *nudging gently in the*
> *tide.*

In thinking of why John Logan's poems are moving, I haven't even mentioned the most obvious reason— the marvelous openness in them, the way he talks directly of his loneliness, his prayers, the decay of the body, his divorce and his children, his disappointments or failures. This openness is new to poetry of the last thirty years, and Allen Ginsberg and James Wright in differing ways have done a lot to encourage it. The so-called Confessional Poets have also. Yet something mysterious is involved. We notice that sometimes a "Confessional Poet" confesses in a poem faults more horrendous than anything Logan or Wright confesses and we are not moved at all. Most underground newspaper poetry is not moving either, although it's open. So openness is not poetry in itself, unless something else—maybe body sound—is there.

John Logan is suffering the anguish of the body. He is sensitive to its instinctual shifts, and the magnetic energies of the body intelligence. He follows the patterns in a zigzag dance, like the capillaries moving through the flesh, or the heavy-masted ship in the wind.

1961, 1971

PART THREE

Educating
the Rider
and the Horse

Form in Society
and in the Poem

I

It seems that a feeling of constriction was habitual in the nineteenth century. To judge by literature, people felt a sense of constriction in the streets, in drawing rooms, and inside their heads. Jane Austen focused on it in the English country home; Dickens, in the streets. Rimbaud describes the thousand ways he felt restrained and hemmed in: he was suffocated by his boring town, the alexandrine line, the stuffy subject matter, the stanza; he rebels against his family, the Second Empire, "ideas," the literary society, and Europe. Such rebellion was a conjuring act that often took away the feeling of constriction, which was both political and literary. A rebel against certain forms in poetry was usually also a rebel against the aristocratic and bourgeois conventions. Whitman is a good example. He fought against the old poetic forms, bringing free verse, and also announced the end of class in society, the coming of brotherhood. The whole rebellious and iconoclastic tradition of the nineteenth century, continuing through Ibsen and Laforgue, emerges I think from this feeling of constriction, felt every day in the consciousness.

In the twentieth century we are half-conscious that too many babies are being born on earth, cities are expanding out of control, businesses join, publishers merge, corporations grow bigger and bigger. Even idea systems expand: industrialists become interested in blacks and have liberal viewpoints, Continental Can supports Plato, old lefties work for *The National Review*— the living room of the mind widens to include other cultures, other galaxies. Everyone wants to be in a gaseous instead of a solid, state. The Wall Street broker is troubled, like his peyote-chewing foil, by the expansion of his own ego, which seems nearly ready to fill the whole universe. This mood of uncontrollable expansion troubles us, just as its opposite, the mood of constriction, troubled those living in the nineteenth century.

II

Our attitude toward expansion is ambiguous. The administration encourages expansion in business, but wants countries like Cuba to stay in their place. Ministers expand their churches, but dislike expansion in corporations. The American middle class senses an evil in expansion, but its attitude is confused. Allen Ginsberg, who is an intelligent man, embodies the expansion around him in his form, attacks it in his content, calling it "Moloch," and participates in it enthusiastically with his life.

That solution is characteristic: we feel troubled, but

like the jazzy way of life and don't want to give it up. We end up praising it.

A person who praises what is destroying him can believe anything. We want to believe that American expansiveness is good, and so the most impossible thoughts on the subject of freedom and order are spoken and accepted. Many people have declared that drug use is freedom. Monopoly is free enterprise. Armies are for peace. The secretary of state says that Honduras is a part of the free world.

III

In the nineteenth century the poet said, "Watch me. I have broken the forms in my poem, and the poetry remains. Do the same. Break the forms in community and the essence of community will remain." Rimbaud took this step, Whitman also. The essence of poetry remained when people broke forms, but the essence of community did not. In poetry, Yvor Winters and several contemporary followers advise us to reimpose old form. That may be all right. But we know from the experience of Germany and Italy in this century that modern society cannot be made livable by the reimposition of old forms.

Because the sense of constriction has come to an end, fruitful emphasis on freeing poetry from constriction has ended. All the work on overcoming constriction is no longer helpful, and critics in poetry and society are not agreed on how to approach expansion.

We know that some political leaders have been able to live out their infinite hungers by slipping past the old restraints of Parliament, custom, separation of powers, checks and balances. Hitler is an example—how easily he dissolved the German parliament. The so-called Savings and Loan scandal in the United States is another political example. The Congress removes "regulation" and instantly the owners of Savings and Loans fall into expansive grandiosity, and the loss expands to billions.

To return to the poem, we can say that the counting of beats in Anglo-Saxon poetry, the obligatory pause, the careful attention to opening consonants, the use of elaborate kennings and back references to old stories regulated and laid restraints on grandiosity. Poems that express opposing points of view, such as Yeats' "Dialogue of Self and Soul," amount to restraints on grandiosity; the purely lyric poem, by contrast—which expresses one point of view only—does not put any holds on infantile grandiosity. Milan Kundera complains that "the lyric poet always identifies himself with his feelings." From Kundera's point of view then, "the unbearable lightness of being" is precisely this lyrical expansionism, with no discrepancy between what things believe they are and what they are.

IV

Something in us wants and wants endlessly. Witches and giants in fairy stories stand for that wanting. The witch wants a ton of wheat sorted in an hour, she wants all the fish in the river to be laid out by species and in neat rows this afternoon; the giant wants to eat now, now, now, and he can eat for days, he can eat all the food produced in the county this year. Goya's painting of Saturn eating his son suggests the anguish inseparable from that endless, repetitive, abusing hunger.

Kohut and the self psychologists have named the source of this infinite hunger infantile grandiosity or psychological omnipotence. When a two- or three-year-old child is on the grandiose road, it has godlike goals and is not at all sure that it is not God. Limits, conditions, bounds, confines are something the child doesn't want to hear of. Alice Miller remarks that each person chooses either the grandiose road or the depressed road; but, of course, inside each depressed person there is a grandiose person, and vice versa. It is infantile grandiosity that destroys the forests without counting the cost and pollutes the lakes. Longing for the infinite is at the root of American consumption of drugs, and policemen cannot help with that.

Whitman then is justly the American poet. He solved contradiction by expanding, and he did find the godlike. So Whitman is both authentically mystical and authentically infantile.

Our task here is not to point fingers, for the fingers would simply curve and point at us—author and reader alike—but to work toward an understanding of the grandiosity that has eroded both poetry and society in the twentieth century.

Side by side with the surrealist poetry of extreme lightness in the United States is the poetry of flatness. Kohut's thought applies to this artistic problem. He believes that the godlike omnipotence inside the adult person, preserved from early childhood, troubles him or her; its omnipotence, even though curtailed and driven back by parents, schoolmates, driving instructors, and priests, remains inside, cooking. The omnipotence has an open channel, never broken, to the infinite heat of

God's room, which we can imagine as the Castle of Stromberg, the White Bear's mansion, the realm of archetypes, or the reaction chambers of the physical sun. Some people who are terrified of grandiosity spend their vital energy defending themselves from the godlike furnace cooking inside them. They are the flat people. Side by side with the light poetry we have the flat poetry of the universities, flatter than any poetry ever known in the world before. In the first the poet gives association haphazardly, and ascends out of sight; in the second the poet resists association, sticks to the facts, and receives his certificate in genuine nongrandiosity.

Providing associative poetry without emotional content is a technique of the ascenders; reimposing traditional meter is a technique of the flat people. Neither should be rejected, but there must be a third way. It lies in a poetry that keeps its connection to wildness, to grandiosity, and to mythological magnificence, and at the same time builds into the lines the planned pitches, the pauses, the sound-repetitions that the Anglo-Saxon poets used to support and regulate their wildness. The subject to some degree would be grandiosity itself. And the rhythms would be depressed. Limits enter in that way. The mood would be proper to our failures. Then the poet could say to society: "I have broken my grandiosity, and the essence of the human remains."

1961, 1990

The Dead World
and the Live World

I

A new point of view allows the traveler to see deep into certain valleys. What we want to look into here is the landscape dominated by John Updike, Arthur Miller, Saul Bellow—the American literary landscape at the moment. For point of view, let us take a contrast, not too often talked of, between two sorts of literature: between poetry that is locked inside the ego and poetry that reaches out in waves over everything that is alive.

Some writers bring us "news of the human mind." Arthur Miller is a perfect example. To say that nature was missing in his work would be an understatement—what is missing is microbes, gods, oceans; what is missing is the universe.

The Heart of Darkness is different. *The Heart of Darkness*, like the poems of Roethke and Whitman, brings us "news of the universe." Conrad takes us inside a human mind, but when we get there it turns out we are deep inside a continent. We feel the immensity of nature, how much of it is beyond the ego. "Once, I remember, we came upon a man-of-war, anchored off the coast . . . the muzzles of the long six-inch guns stuck out all over the low hull. . . . In the empty immensity of earth, sky, and water, there she was, incomprehensible, firing into a continent." Conrad is not analyzing his neighbor; he is trying to get some understanding of the interdependence of all the beings in the world.

The aim of the literature that studies primarily human beings was well phrased by Pope: "The proper study of mankind is man." Encouraged by the egocentricity of St. Paul, it studies the human mind as if it were cut off from the rest of the universe. Writers of this kind regard the "I" as something independent, isolated, entire in itself, and they throw themselves into studying its turns and impulses.

The psychoanalyst Georg Groddeck, in an essay called "*Charakter und Typus*," written about 1907, gives Goethe as a supreme example of the writer who "brings us news of the universe." He quotes Goethe's short poem "*Wandrers Nachtlied*":

> *There is a stillness*
> *On the tops of the hills.*
> *In the tops of the trees*
> *you feel*
> *hardly a breath.*
> *The little birds fall silent in the boughs.*
> *Simply wait: soon*
> *You too will be still.*

He says that "Goethe's short poems have a very strange ring to them. They are entirely impersonal; in fact, you could say of them that they are not created by a person but by nature. In them a person is not seen as an 'I' but as a part of something else."

The "human" poets study the three classic faculties: feeling, will, and intellect. The poets of the universe accept these faculties, and are aware of an additional energy inside themselves. Groddeck calls this energy the "*Gott-natur*." The *Gott-natur* senses the interdependence of all things alive and longs to bring them all inside a work of art. The work of these poets is an elaborate expression of the *Gott-natur*. What results is a calmness.

II

Groddeck noticed that European literature after about 1600 had taken a curious path: it had gradually allowed itself to be dominated by writers without *Gott-natur*, by literature engrossed in aggressively human reactions. He mentioned Shakespeare, Pope, Kleist, Byron, the domestic dramas of Ibsen and Shaw. In the nineteenth century, the tradition became bankrupt. European drama, poetry, fiction, music, and painting had by 1900, he says, all driven themselves into a dead end. James Joyce's *Ulysses* was not written until some years after Groddeck's essay, but it is the perfect example in fiction of the exhausted ego-art Groddeck foresaw. *Ulysses* is human in a poverty-stricken way, and tries to make the ordinary person into something epic by exhaustive psychological and literary detail.

In European painting, both impressionism and expressionism were successful attempts to break the hold of this ego-art. The painters broke it decisively after 1900—more decisively than the writers did. Our view of the "modern movement" in literature is confused because we have never tried to distinguish the works that were products of the dying tradition, like *Ulysses*, from those that came into being precisely to break the dying tradition. *Ulysses* is part of the dead world; Trakl's poems are part of the live world. Hoddis, Rilke, Machado, Redon, and Max Ernst also belong to the live world.

III

Suppose a country's literature never does shed its skin, what will happen to it? Suppose it doesn't move on to anything new, but instead insists, like Snodgrass in *Heart's Needle*, or Lowell in *Life Studies*, on studying the exclusively human over and over? Suppose also that the human being is not studied in relation to nonhuman lives, or lives in other countries, but simply in relation to itself? One can predict first of all that such a nation will bomb foreign populations very easily, because it has no sense of anything real beyond its own ego. What direction the literature will take is not so easy to predict. Groddeck, however, attempts it. He says the literature of such a nation will take refuge in the sensational.

The writers will all be small Beethovens.

"They write of what is out of the ordinary, they make their art from extreme mental states. This is of course quite understandable. Only a person with really sluggish blood could put up with the average interior state of the human being without yawning, and to make art out of

it is impossible, at least not in the way Shakespeare or Beethoven go about it. . . . The only poet who could make anything out of it is a man who sees in human beings a part of the universe, for whom human nature is interesting not because it is human, but because it is nature. Goethe could do that, Bach also. However, if an artist has no Gott-natur in him—and one finds this nature these days most often in men who are intellectually silent, very seldom in those who have gone through schools—then he has no choice but to buckle knee-length buskins on his characters. By doing that he makes them more appealing. In other words, he **has** *to look for something* **extreme;** *and if it isn't there, he will insert it into his characters by* **force:** *he* **has** *to be romantic."*

IV

How much that sounds like Plath, Sextor, or Lowell! Arthur Miller some time ago gave up ordinary salesmen and now reaches for characters that are psychologically extreme like Marilyn Monroe. Truman Capote took that road in *In Cold Blood.* For the confessional poet anything less than a divorce or a nervous breakdown doesn't justify the machinery. A poem becomes a tank that can't maneuver on soft ground without destroying it.

Although the impressionist and expressionist movements broke the hold of this dying school in European painting, and the expressionist and Freudian movements broke its hold in poetry, the exhausted traditions stagger on in self-complacent America, greeted with wild cries. We seem to have no clear idea of any other tradition *but* this one. Instead of trying to break it up, our serious critics help to maintain it. The intellectual bankruptcy of *The New York Review of Books* lies precisely in its confinement to the dying tradition. Norman Mailer, a hardworking latecomer, tries the best he can to be extreme.

V

I am not criticizing these writers for being interested in human beings. When a man talks of the human because he is leaping out toward it—Paracelsus said, "The love of God will be kindled in our hearts by an ardent love of humanity"—then humanity becomes something luminous. But when writers talk hysterically about the human because of failure of imagination and emotional exhaustion; when they can think of nothing else that is exciting, when they are *reduced* to the human—then what is human is barren. I am not urging a nature poetry either, but rather a poetry that goes deep into the human being, much deeper than the ego, and at the same time is aware of trees and angels. The confessional poets tend to believe that the human being is something extremely important *in itself*. That is why they are always telling us every fact about their operations. Poets of this sort will accept calmly the extinction of the passenger pigeon or the blue whale. These are the poets to whom Nerval was talking when he suddenly turned and said, "When you gather to plan, the universe is not there."

VI

Groddeck believed that Western writers had abandoned *Gott-natur* for centuries and only now were beginning to have the strength to pick it up again. Yeats expressed similar ideas in his essays. Certainly a sense of *Gott-natur* stands at the very center of ecological work, and the poets around it, for example, Gary Snyder, Wendell Berry, and Annie Dillard, among many others. A feeling for *Gott-natur* stands at the center of Joseph Campbell's work as well. If in literature we put human concerns above all else, we continue "firing into a continent." When we are planning a work of poetry or fiction, it is just to hope that the universe will be present.

1966

Intense States
of Consciousness

American artists have begun to lose their morale. The American Indian knew he had gone through a disastrous change in the late nineteenth century; he found he had "lost his dreams." The dreams of sacred muskrats or of white stallions with the colors of the four directions painted on their flanks, stopped coming. When he woke up in the morning, his mind was blank. The visual artists in the United States, at least much of the New York school, have already lost their dreams. Pop art represents not the *presence* of something, but the absence of a great dream.

A great dream is by definition private, even secret, as Leonardo felt his dreams to be; a dream dreamed by many people is not a dream but an obsession.

Novelists have lost some of their faith in the power of imagination and fantasy lately and edge over steadily toward nonfiction or in-between forms such as the fictional documentary.

Poetry still retains its spirit, and the poets in the United States (and in Russia) have added to their spirit in the last decade. American poets have led the national writers in public opposition to the Vietnam War. The novelists have been less active, and the dramatists almost invisible.

I think the reason for a certain lameness in the novelists is that fiction in the West has traditionally been written in an ordinary state of consciousness. We imagine the novelist to be, like Thomas Mann, satisfied with bourgeois life and a steady laborer (he knocks out a certain number of words every day). Creative writing courses have, willy-nilly, supported the view that an ordinary state of consciousness is all right for serious writing.

But that's not so. Twentieth-century life (compared, for instance, to eighteenth-century life in Europe) is so intense, so soaked with unconscious or half-conscious substance, so deeply impelled by psychic energies desperately attempting to get loose, that it cannot be understood in an ordinary state of consciousness. The massive failure of middle-aged politicians in all countries testifies to that, as does the spectacular failure of so many educational, artistic, and welfare efforts in recent years.

The New Age obsessions with occult thought, expanding consciousness, and body-mind connections spring from an awareness that the old state of consciousness can guide them only into the swamp where their parents have been and where the Marines now are.

Poetry in the United States now has considerable and increasing energy, both political and private, and readers who recognize poetry's connection with earth and soul. Gary Snyder's work, for example, feels essential to ecologists, Buddhists, antinuclear activists, and thousands of ordinary readers. Something similar can be said of Kinnell, Levertov, William Stafford. The contemporary poets in general have not lost their morale, that is, their faith in imagination and in intense states of consciousness. Poetry has not lost its "dream," and so can oppose that dream to the hooded longings in the barbarian national psyche, lighting up both, providing a sudden background, as lightning does in a night storm.

The problem of poetry now is to find ways to go into still more intense states of consciousness. Its daily helpers in this will be discipline and solitude. Its intellectual helpers will be writers like Thoreau, Marcuse, Norman Brown, Akhmatova, and Vallejo. It will address itself to those who sooner or later will have to imagine a new start in the inner life of the West, for the way we are following is a disaster.

1968

Leaping Up
into Political Poetry

I

Poems that touch on American history usually have political implications. But most critics believe that poetry on political subjects should not be attempted. For an intricate painting, we are urged to bring forward our finest awareness. At the same time, we understand that we should leave that awareness behind when we go to examine political acts. Our wise men and wise institutions assure us that national political events are beyond the reach of ordinary, or even extraordinary, literary sensitivity.

That habit is not new: Thoreau's friends thought that his writings on nature were very good, but that he was beyond his depth when he protested against the Mexican War. The circumstances surrounding the Austrian Franz Jagerstätter, whose life ended thirty years ago, during World War II, are very interesting in this connection. Jagerstätter was a farmer, with the equivalent of a high-school education, although he possessed a remarkable intelligence. He decided that the Nazis were incompatible with the best he had seen and read of life, and he made this decision before the Nazis took over in Austria; he cast the only no ballot in his village against the Anschluss. Jagerstätter's firm opposition to the Nazi regime is particularly interesting because he did not act out a doctrinaire position of a closely knit group, like the Jehovah's Witnesses, nor was he a member of a group being systematically wiped out, like the Jews: he simply made up his mind on a specific political situation, relying on his own judgment and what he was able to piece together from the Bible, and using information available to everyone.

When drafted by the Nazis after the Anschluss, he refused to serve. The military judges sympathized, but told him they would have to kill him if he did not change his mind. Gordon Zahn's book, *In Solitary Witness*, recounts the meeting Jagerstätter had with various authorities shortly before his execution. All persons in authority who interviewed Jagerstätter, including bishops of the Austrian Catholic Church, psychiatrists, lawyers, and judges, told him that his sensibility was advising him wrongly. He was not responsible for acts he might take as a soldier: that was the responsibility of the legal government. They told him that he should turn his sensibility to the precarious situation of his family. He was advised, in effect, not to be serious. It was recommended that he be Christian in regard to his domestic life, but not to his political life. Jagerstätter's studies had increased the range of his sensibility, and now this sensibility looked on acts he would have to take under orders by the government with the same calm penetration with which it would look on wasting time, or deciding on the quality of a book. He had extended his awareness further than society wanted him to; and everyone he met, with the exception of a single parish priest, tried to drive it back again. Jagerstätter, however, refused to change his mind, would not enter the army, and was executed.

Most Americans have serious doubts about the morality of the Vietnam War. We are all aware of the large number of spirited and courageous young Americans in the resistance who are refusing induction and are risking and being given lengthy prison sentences.

The majority of American draftees, however, go into the army as they are told. Their doubt is interrupted on its way, and does not continue forward to end in an act, as Jagerstätter's doubt did or as the objector's and resister's doubt does. This failure to carry through means essentially that American culture has succeeded in killing some sensibilities. In order to take the rebellious and responsible action, the man thinking must be able to establish firm reasons for it; and in order to imagine those reasons, his awareness must have grown, over years, finer and finer. The "invisible organs of government," schools, broadcasting houses, orthodox churches, move to kill the awareness. The schools emphasize competitiveness over compassion; television and advertising do their part in numbing the sensibilities. Killing awareness is easier than killing the man later for a firm act.

II

The calculated effort of a society to kill awareness helps to explain why so few citizens take rebellious actions.

But I'm not sure it explains why so few American poets have written political poems. A poem can be a political act, but it has not been, so far at least, an illegal act. Moreover, because much of the poet's energy goes toward extending his awareness, he is immune to the more gross effects of brainwashing. Why then have so few American poems penetrated to any reality in our political life? I think one reason is that political concerns and inward concerns have always been regarded in our tradition as opposites, even incompatibles. *Time* is very upset that Buddhists should take part in political activity: the *Time* writers are convinced that the religious and political worlds are mutually exclusive, and if you work in one, you are excused from working in the other. English and American poets have adopted this schema also, and poets in the fifties felt that in *not* writing anything political, they were doing something meritorious. It's clear that many of the events that create our foreign relations and our domestic relations come from more or less hidden impulses in the American psyche. It's also clear, I think, that some sort of husk has grown around that psyche, so that in the fifties we could not look into it or did not. The friction of the civil rights movement and the Vietnam War have worn the husk thin in a couple of places now. But if that is so, then the poet's main job is to penetrate that husk around the American psyche, and because that psyche is inside *him* too, the writing of political poetry is like the writing of personal poetry, a sudden drive by the poet inward.

As a matter of fact, we notice that it has been inward poets, such as Robert Duncan, Denise Levertov, and Galway Kinnell, who have written the best poems about the Vietnam War.

When a poet succeeds in driving partway inward, he often develops new energy that carries him on through the polished husk of the inner psyche that deflects most citizens and poets. Once inside the psyche, he can speak of inward and political things with the same assurance. We can make a statement then that would not have been accepted in the thirties, namely, that what is needed to write good poems about the outward world is inwardness. The political activists in the literary world are wrong—they try to force political poetry out of poets by pushing them more deeply into events, making them feel guilt if they don't abandon privacy. But the truth is that the political poem comes out of the deepest privacy.

III

Let me continue a minute with the comparison of the political poem with the personal poem. I'll use Yeats's marvelous word "entangle"; he suggests that the symbolist poem entangles some substance from the divine world in its words. Similarly a great personal poet like Villon entangles some of the private substance of his life in his language so well that hundreds of years later it still remains embedded. The subject of personal poetry is often spiritual growth, or the absence of it.

The dominant poem in American literature has always been the personal poem. John Crowe Ransom, for instance, wrote an elegant version of the personal poem; Randall Jarrell, a flabby version; Robert Lowell, a harsh version; Reed Whittemore, a funny version; W. D. Snodgrass, a whining version; Robert Creeley, a laconic one; and so forth. I love the work of many of these poets, but they choose, on the whole, not to go beyond the boundaries of the personal poem. Many poets say flatly—and proudly—that they are "not political." If a tree said that, I would find it more convincing than when a man says it. I think it is conceivable that a tree could report that it grew just as well in the Johnson administration as in the Kennedy administration or the Lincoln administration. But a modern man's spiritual life and his growth are increasingly sensitive to the tone and content of a regime. A man of draft age will find that his life itself depends on the political content of an administration. So these poets' assertion of independence is, I think, a fiction.

The only body of political poetry written with any determination in the United States was written during the thirties by Edwin Rolfe, Sol Funaroff, Kenneth Fearing, Muriel Rukeyser, and other left-wing poets. It is interesting that their poems were usually political in *opinion*. For example, the poet might declare that he had discovered who is robbing whom. But he usually doesn't grasp intuitively that there might be a robber inside him. These political poems of the thirties then were not really poems at all, but opinions. We find in the sixties many political poems still made up of opinions; they are political all right but not poems. For example, the poet might say,

> *Poor America*
> *so huge, so strong, so afraid.*
> *afraid in Guatemala,*
> *afraid in Congo, Panama,*
> *afraid in Cuba, in Santo Domingo,*

afraid in Vietnam . . .
America, take your hands off Vietnam!
The poor are rising
You are through stealing now
Your face is distorted with hate . . .

These lines have boiled up from the outermost layer of
the brain. The poem is not inside the poet's own life,
let alone inside this nation's life.

The life of the nation can be imagined also not as
something deep inside our psyche, but as a psyche
larger than the psyche of anyone living, a larger sphere,
floating above everyone. In order for the poet to write
a true political poem, he has to be able to have such a
grasp of his own concerns that he can leave them for a
while and then leap up into this other psyche. He wanders about there for a while and, as he returns, he brings
back plant seeds that have stuck to his clothes, some
inhabitants of this curious sphere, which he then tries
to keep alive with his own psychic body.

Some poets try to write political poems impelled by
hatred or fear. But these emotions are heavy, they affect
the gravity of the body. What the poet needs to get up
that far and bring back something are great leaps of the
imagination.

A true political poem is a quarrel with ourselves, and
the rhetoric is as harmful in that sort of poem as in the
personal poem. The true political poem does not order
us either to take any specific acts: like the personal
poem, it moves to deepen awareness.

Thinking of the rarity of the political poem in the
United States, another image comes to mind. We can
imagine Americans inside a sphere, like those sad men

in Bosch's "Garden of Earthly Delights." The clear glass is the limit of the ego. We float inside it. Around us there are worlds of energy, but we are unable to describe them in words, because we are unable to get out of our own egos.

IV

The political poem needs an especially fragrant language. Neruda's "The Dictators" has that curious fragrance that comes from its words brushing unknown parts of the psyche. It seems to me a masterpiece of the political poem:

> An odor has remained among the sugar cane:
> A mixture of blood and body, a penetrating
> Petal that brings nausea.
> Between the coconut palms the graves are full
> Of ruined bones, of speechless death-rattles.
> A delicate underling converses
> With glasses, braid collars, and cords of gold.
> The tiny palace gleams like a watch
> And the rapid laughs with gloves on
> Cross the corridors at times
> And join the dead voices
> And the blue mouths freshly buried.
> The weeping is hidden like a water-plant
> Whose seeds fall constantly on the earth
> And without light make the great blind leaves to grow.
> Hatred has grown scale upon scale,
> Blow on blow, in the ghastly water of the swamp,
> With a snout full of ooze and silence.

Neruda's task is to entangle in the language the psychic substance of a South American country under a dictator. The Spanish original, of course, is much more resonant. But even in the translation it is clear that Neruda is bringing in unexpected images: "The tiny palace gleams like a watch"—images one would expect in an entirely different sort of poem: "rapid laughs with gloves on." Suddenly a blind plant appears, that reproduces itself by dropping seeds constantly on the ground, shaded by its own huge leaves. This image is complicated, created by a part of the mind inaccessible to hatred, and yet it carries the reality of hatred radiating from dictators into the consciousness with a kind of massive intelligence.

Describing dictators in "The United Fruit Company," Neruda uses the image of ordinary houseflies. By contrast, the journalistic mind would tend to describe them as huge and cunning monsters. Whitman was the first true political poet we had in North America. His short poem "To the States" has great fragrance in its language as well.

> *Why reclining, interrogating? why myself and all*
> *drowsing?*
> *What deepening twilight—scum floating atop of*
> *the waters,*
> *Who are they as bats and night-dogs askant in*
> *the capitol?*
> *What a filthy Presidentiad! (O South, your*
> *torrid suns! O North, your arctic freezings!)*
> *Are those really Congressmen; are those the great*
> *Judges? is that the President?*

> *Then I will sleep awhile yet, for I see that these*
> *States sleep, for reasons;*
> *(With gathering murk, with muttering thunder*
> *and lambent shoots we all duly awake,*
> *South, North, East, West, inland and seaboard,*
> *we will surely awake).*

William Vaughn Moody in 1898 wrote some powerful lines:

> *Are we the eagle nation Milton saw*
> *Mewing its mighty youth,*
> *Soon to possess the mountain winds of truth,*
> *And be swift familiar of the sun*
> *Where aye before God's face his trumpets run?*
> *Or have we but the talons and the maw,*
> *And for the abject likeness of our heart*
> *Shall some less lordly bird be set apart?*
> *Some gross-billed wader where the swamps are fat?*
> *Some gorger in the sun? Some prowler with the bat?*

His poem was written against United States policy the first time we invaded Cuba. The language at times is remarkably swift and intense, particularly when compared to the foggy poetry being written by others at that time.

The political poem in the United States after Whitman and Moody lay dormant until the inventive generation of 1917 came along, who revived it with mixed results. Pound demanded that American history enter his *Cantos*; Eliot wrote well, although always of a generalized modern nation, rather than of the United States; Jeffers wrote marvelously, but really disliked the United States as a nation. During the forties the New Critical mentality, profoundly opposed to any questioning of the white power structure, took over, and the language and strength of political poetry survived in William Carlos Williams and in three younger poets, Kenneth Rexroth, Thomas McGrath, and David Ignatow. During the forties and fifties most poets kept away from the political poem. In his "Ode for the American Dead in Korea," Thomas McGrath wrote,

> *And God (whose sparrows fall aslant his gaze,*
> *Like grace or confetti) blinks, and he is gone,*
> *And you are gone . . . But, in another year*
> *We will mourn you, whose fossil courage fills*
> *The limestone histories: brave: ignorant: amazed:*
> *Dead in the rice paddies, dead on the nameless hills.*

Rexroth has written beautiful political poems, among them "A Christmas Note for Geraldine Udell." His great common sense and stubborn intelligence helped immensely in keeping the political poem alive.

The influence of the New Criticism in poetry began to dim in the middle 1950s, just at the time America's fantastic capacity for aggression and self-delusion began to be palpable like rising water to the beach walker. William Carlos Williams's refusal to ignore political lies was passed on to Allen Ginsberg; Neruda's example began to take hold; Rexroth, McGrath, and Ignatow continued to write well; Ferlinghetti separately wrote his "A Tentative Description of a Dinner Given to Promote the Impeachment of President Eisenhower." Many black poets such as Leroi Jones and Robert Hayden began to be visible. As the Vietnam War escalated, Robert

Duncan wrote several powerful poems on the war. His "Uprising" ends:

> *this specter that in the beginning Adams and*
> *   Jefferson feared and knew*
> *would corrupt the very body of the nation*
> *   and all our sense of our common humanity . . .*
> *now shines from the eyes of the President*
> *   in the swollen head of the nation.*

America is still young herself, and she may become something magnificent and shining, or she may turn, as Rome did, into a black dinosaur, the enemy of every nation in the world who wants to live its own life. In my opinion, that decision has not yet been made.

1968

Where Have All
the Critics Gone?

I'm going to make a few remarks on the disappearance of New Criticism, and after that disappearance, the fading of the whole profession of public criticism, which was once a fruitful way for a man or woman to use his or her intelligence.

When we read the magazines, we *feel* there is little criticism around. In fact, a new book of poetry published in the last decade may get only one or two reviews. Reviews appear, but with not much energy. Obviously, too many books get printed. A critic then reviews his friend's new book, to make sure it gets at least one review, and as that happens, fewer critics look dispassionately at the whole spectrum. *APR*, the tabloid *American Poetry Review*, does not cover the spectrum. Instead of running reviews that might cause dissension, *APR* prints a twenty-page article simply patting the feathers of some established poet, articles so boring that even graduate students can't read them without weeping. There is something sheeplike in criticism: one year everyone reviews Ashbery, but no one reviews Rukeyser or Rexroth or Logan. The big review places don't do enough, but the little magazines are just as bad. Whole issues appear with poems on every page, and not one review; and the editor feels "more creative" doing that. *The Nation, The New Republic,* and *The New York Times Book Review* do moderately well in reviewing poetry, compared to certain times in the past, but everywhere the huge amount of poetry being published simply swamps the criticism printed.

More and more books of poetry are appearing, more and more of them supported by grants from the National Foundation for the Arts and Humanities. This artificial priming, or governmental interference, is having bad effects. The grants now support magazines that would otherwise mercifully have died. If you're an editor, and you're putting out an issue on time *to get your grant,* the easiest thing is to fill it with poems. If they're bad, you say, "At least I'm helping the poet to get started!" It's less trouble than printing criticism. First of all, printing reviews involves assigning the books, correspondence with the writer, mailing the books, checking the prose, and besides, reviews bring you enemies. Who knows but that the best friend of the poet you just attacked may be on the board of the National Endowment grants? Maybe he is the nephew of your department chairman? A few little magazines persistently print lively criticism; *Ironwood* comes to mind, *Kayak, Parnassus, Georgia Review,* but most criticism is done verbally, and not set down except in theses buried in libraries.

We have an odd situation: although more bad poetry is being published now than ever before in American history, most of the reviews are positive. Critics say, "I never attack what is bad, all that will take care of itself," or "Life is too short to spend time on what is no good;

I only write about what I like." That would be nice if we were all gods, but the country is full of young poets and readers who are confused by seeing mediocre poetry praised, or never attacked, and who end up doubting their own critical perceptions. When the older writers remain silent on what they despise, the younger ones get confused. The emphasis on praising everything is part of the sixties, and its odd belief that criticism is an attempt to put down the young or minorities. This is condescending to young poets and no help to anyone. Younger poets are considered tender blooms, whom a harsh word will wither. Everyone becomes a minority.

This overindulgence follows from the most serious disturbance in poetry of the last thirty years—the emergence of "poetry workshops" in the universities. The other day Wendell Berry said to me, "I'm disturbed about poetry becoming a commodity. Robert, there are no poetry teachers left in this country!" I asked him what he meant, and he spoke of how teachers in this country tend to conduct their workshops in a way that ensures they'll receive support from the students. "That is not teaching." Good teaching clearly throws the student against the wall. Before workshops, young modern poets learned by comparing their poems to Yeats's, and that was very depressing. Yeats did not comfort them. The Chinese have a story of a teacher who overturned his student in a boat, and whenever the student put his head above the water, the teacher poked him under with a long pole. That's very different from granting MFAs. The University of Iowa workshop under Justice and Bell is famous for this overencouragement, especially of the like-minded.

We all love encouragement, so the students receive

their MFAs, and then overencourage their students in return, or become editors who don't judge but encourage. Allen Ginsberg once said something true about this. A reporter at a poetry conference, I think in Vancouver, asked him if he and the other teachers had taught the principles of American prosody. "No," Allen said, "we were all bankrupt and ran around weeping, asking the students for love." I don't mean that this is what happens at Iowa or Amherst or the Naropa poetry workshops, always, or at all workshops anytime, but I think that a teacher of writing to be good has to have enough love so that he doesn't ask it from his students. Even poets like me who don't teach tend to ask the audience at a poetry reading for love, and that's no good either.

The overencouragement that one feels in Naropa, in Iowa, in Montana, in Amherst leads to similar beneficence in reviewing. It has even risen to the highest levels of critical theory. Harold Bloom, an intelligent man, differs from his critical colleagues of thirty years ago, such as Edmund Wilson or Ivor Winters, in that he refuses to look at the broad spectrum of what is coming out and do the critic's job, which is to separate the rotten grain from the sound, without fear of being wrong and without implied approval by silence. Wilson did that well in fiction; Ehrenpreis does it once in a while in poetry now. But Bloom chooses instead a couple of favorite poets—in his case A. R. Ammons and John Ashbery—and feels his responsibility to contemporary poetry is fulfilled by elevating them. Their poetry deserves praise, but somehow the whole project is wrong in mood and results, and sets a poor example for other critics. The poets in return tend to dedicate their books to Bloom, and then where is harsh old Edmund Wilson? Nowhere. Ammons and Ashbery do not need elevation anyway, but criticism, so as to help them move on into something new.

I believe very much in the community providing, now and then, the kick that helps the wheel to keep turning. We all have more in us than comes out. Harold Bloom teaches poets to wrestle with dead fathers; but it seems to me that it is important for poets to wrestle with, even attack, living fathers and living sons. My own generation of poets, Kinnell, Snyder, Rich, Levertov, Simpson, Ginsberg, Hall, Merwin, Stafford, and others, has not been attacked enough by younger poets. Being rude to older poets is just a way of clearing ground for yourself. As my remarks make clear, I believe in a healthy pugnacity in criticism.

I have one more idea on the disappearance of criticism as a provocative activity, and that is that "creativity" in the United States is considered to raise one above the working class. Receiving an MFA does not certify you as a poet—no one can do that—but it certifies that you are no longer a blue-collar person. Of course, we are then grateful to the Lord of the Castle who lifted us out of the beet fields. So these Empires of Mutual Affection or empires of like-sounding poets produced at Iowa or St. Marks resemble those parties of governmental officials in Chekhov or Tolstoy, talking quietly, so glad to be able to wear white gloves.

Surely true creativity is linked with revolution, with what Blake calls "Orc" energy. . . . But no revolutionary poetry is coming out of the workshops, no poetry that even touches on political subjects. However, if this MFA "creativity" is a narrow ladder leading out of the working class, how could it be revolutionary?

Impossible. "The climber turns his back to those below."

What I'm suggesting then is that there is a curious link of workshop creativity with white-collar work, and then criticism and the labor of criticism get left behind in the Russian village, with the mud and the pigs. It is "not-desirable" work. How else can you explain the contrast between the wonderful pride in critical intelligence that John Crowe Ransom showed, as well as Parrington and Brooks and Blackmur and Hyman and Wilson, with the shamefaced stuff that comes out now? Where are the critics with a wide sweep, with a joy in their own critical intelligence, and a willingness to be harsh? I see Kenneth Rexroth. I see Susan Sontag. . . . Who else?

I have a practical suggestion, and that is that every person publishing poetry or fiction in this country take a vow to review two books every six months. If the "critics" have lost morale, and are not reappearing in strength, then the poets and novelists will have to do the criticism themselves, ourselves. It's a bit like learning to clean your own house. The servants used to do it. But now we can't wait for a review assignment to come along; we have to assign them to ourselves, and then later see about getting them printed.

In our situation we need poets and writers who are willing to do the hard work around literature, that is, to separate weak work from strong, photography from art. In brief, we need people with a joy in their own intellect and judgment.

1978

The Wheel
of Intelligence

Jung has the idea that inside each of us there are four "intelligences" or ways of grasping the world, and that in each of us, one of the four ways is dominant and the other three present, but in a slave condition. In the typical intellectual the thinking way of grasping the world is on top, but this in turn means that the feeling side is on the bottom. Jung once gave a talk in English, describing this system, to a group of psychiatrists in London, most of whom, he surmised, were intellectuals. That means, he said, that in your thinking ability you are perhaps fifty-two; in your feeling about thirteen. When you go home at night, your wife meets a thirteen year old.

The four-intelligence system is visualized as a circle with the dominant function, in our example, thinking, in the north position, and its complement, feeling, in the underneath or south position. In every person there are also two "wing functions," thrown out to the side, ways of grasping the world that are neither strong nor weak, which we can visualize in the east and west positions. The third function is the ability to grasp physical fact; facing that is its opposite, intuition, the ability to grasp possibilities in the invisible world. The power to grasp physical facts, to know that a table is made of good wood, that a barn can hold ten tons of hay, to know how many blacks and whites vote in a given area is a power useful to the farmer, the businessman, and the politician, in whom this mode of intelligence will often be dominant. Dreiser is a classic example of the writer with his grasp of fact developed beyond other modes. Intuition sees the shape and size of objects *inside* the unconscious, it sees the hidden links between the "ghosts of things" and the things themselves. Rilke is clearly a writer of this sort, who saw objects in the unconscious with astounding detail and also had considerable gift as a medium. A medium or "sensitive," whose intuition has been developed far above all other modes of intelligence, is able to guess from one image she sees in your unconscious where you were born, how many children you have, what sort of inner path you walk; we notice, however, that shapes and uses of objects in the outer world are often vague to the medium. Intuitive intelligence feels forward into possibility, and such intelligence often finds "the way things actually are" boring.

The circle may be turned so that any one of the modes is on top, and its opposite on the bottom. In Robert Frost, whose grasp of physical fact was so marvelous, the intuitive intelligence was not trustworthy, although he worked on it always. He often did the wrong thing in human relations, and, as he said in his poem "Home Burial," he never entirely understood what it was he was doing wrong.

This is the elementary visualization of the four modes. Readers who want a clearer picture of it can read Jung's lectures to the English psychiatrists, published as *Analytical Psychology: Its Theory and Practice*, or they can read his more elaborate book, *Psychological Types*. The concept of the four modes, or ways of grasping the world, leads to a theory of personality types. We have four basic types: the thinking type, in whom feeling is weak and archaic; the feeling type, in whom thinking is stereotyped and undeveloped; the grasp of physical fact type, in whom intuition hardly functions at all; and the intuitive type, whose grasp of the physical world is hazy. I think the general idea is clear, and needs no more detail. The mode of intelligence turned to the bottom, the weaker one, Jung calls the "inferior function" and we will keep that terminology here.

When we turn to poetry, keeping the four intelligences in mind, several rather magical thoughts appear. We are all fond of our dominant function and feel it is our strength, but Jung suspected that we create works of art, including poems, with our inferior function. If a poet's dominant mode is thinking, the poetry will actually be written by the feeling side, which is the weakest part of him or her. That's a very strange idea to me, but it helps to explain why poetry is so erratic in the way it comes: your weakest mode is under the power of all that is latent. One day the poetry is with you, and the next day it is not. The problem with going to school is that the schools pick out the dominant function in any child early and encourage that, at the expense of the others. Such specialization is the way to financial or worldly success, but in the inner life that often means defeat. Certainly it does in art. We all know of successful people who long to paint or write poetry, but cannot do it.

There is a second problem: the typical child of a hierarchical society looks down on what is beneath him or her, on the "inferiors." By a process of association the child, now an adult, looks down on his or her "inferior function," whatever that might be. The university-trained intellectual looks down on his inferior function, feeling, and wants to have nothing to do with it, or not too much. "The blacks have feeling"; he doesn't want that. Similarly the feeling type, sometimes a dancer or a poet, finds ways to dislike thinking . . . he or she feels it is extraneous, it just muddles things, or "those great thinkers run the world, and look at it." The poet in whom intuition is dominant, and who probably likes surrealist poetry, wants only "pure" surrealism, and does not admire details of an actual war. To see that bombs are actually falling is a function of the grasp of facts, which the pure-intuition person disdains as beneath him or her.

It is difficult in a hierarchical society to convince someone to respect his or her inferior function. It was easier for Lawrence, at the "bottom" of English society, to do that than it was for the aristocratic Osbert Sitwell, in whom, as Lawrence saw, the inferior function was entirely paralyzed. (He drew on Sitwell when he made Lady Chattery's aristocratic husband paralyzed from the waist down.) But if the "underneath" is not developed, then there is no poetry, or there is a poetry that dies out while the poet is still in his or her twenties. If that law always applies, it is a hard and mysterious law. It helps to explain why it takes so many years to write poetry. Good poetry can only be written with your weakest function, and even after you discover that, you have to wait years for it to develop. Whitman wrote his first good poem at thirty-five, after his thinking power, which had been weak, developed. Wallace Stevens, I think, was around forty when his first book came out.

A second thought that interests me tremendously—Jung brings the idea up in his English lectures—is this: the inferior function is the link to all the rest of humanity. Your weakest function is like the ground in a radio set. It doesn't make any noise, but through it you pass down into the earth, and so over and up again into humanity. How strange! I always assumed that if a person developed what was strongest in him, that would bring him closer to other people, but I think that Jung is right. Everyone notices that people who have become career successes through developing their dominant function often "lose touch" at a certain point with humanity. "The successful are lonely." Evidently the inferior function remains fairly alive through your twenties. But if a person does not actively care for this function, and consciously develop it after that, it will begin to wither. It is the link with humanity that's withering. Mao Tse-tung talked about it in revolutionary leaders, but surely we see it all around us; in every person we know.

I'll try to relate this system to a few contemporary American poets. We'll start with Louis Simpson. I like Simpson's poetry, and it is extremely rare in its interest in ideas. He draws his title *At the End of the Open Road* from his idea that Whitman's habit of projecting his inner brotherhood on a whole nation was a mistake. "The open road led to the used car lot." I assume that like Stevens he is a poet in whom the thinking function is dominant. We notice that thinking is always about to push feeling out of his poems entirely. I can't prove that, I just sense it when reading the poems. The fact that he makes his living by college teaching probably means he has difficulty developing his weakest function because thinking is relied on in teaching, and feeling is often suspect. One would have to conclude that a poet in whom thinking is dominant should do something else for a living. The feeling function grows stronger in solitude, so the thinking poet should probably be alone a great deal as well. But most of us are alone less in our thirties and forties than in our twenties.

People resist the suggestion that they develop their weaker function—if you suggest that to a thinking type, he'll usually accuse you of wanting him to wallow in feelings. Louis Simpson has accused me of that a number of times; and the early hostility to Allen Ginsberg among thinking-type poets lay in his challenge to them to develop their weak feeling side. In Ginsberg the feeling side is dominant, and he has failed to develop his weak thinking side. This is why he feels lost now, uncertain what to do—sometimes he is ready to stop writing poetry altogether, at other times he wants to continue writing his long epic. The epic, in its constant obsession with American details, telling us that a given gas station is an Esso station, that houses in Kansas are mainly white, that smoke comes out of chimneys, and so forth, means that he is relying on one of his "wing" functions, namely grasp of physical facts. That power is neither weak nor strong in him, neither the conscious nor the unconscious is particularly interested in it; as a result his long poem is boring. One could say that James Tate, despite his immense talent, has failed to develop his inferior thinking power. Tate has given hundreds of poetry readings, but that involves for him relying on his feeling function, which is dominant in him, and so he has the same practical problem as Louis Simpson, but the other way around. Again he makes his living out of his dominant function, and we guess that would inhibit the weak or "fourth" function from growing. In critics the thinking power is usually dominant. Helen Vendler has a well-developed thinking function; her work on Wallace Stevens is often amazingly sharp. Yet when she writes about James Merrill, or another "feeling" poet, she abruptly gives up her dominant power and turns the review over to her undeveloped and rather childish feeling function; then she praises the mediocre for pages. Some women whose main power lies in feeling may overvalue it and be ruthless in depreciating thinking in men or in other women. If a woman has a naturally strong thinking side, her thinking may remind men, curiously, of their undeveloped feeling side, and they dislike it. A man whose thinking function is strongest may choose as a wife a feeling-type woman, whom he allows to do all the feeling for them both. The trade-off is that neither has to experience the pain of psychic growth. It works the other way too: a thinking woman may choose a feeling sort of man and let him do all the feeling.

Much of the poetry we see in magazines is weak because the writer is recognizing only one of his modes and ignoring the rest. In Emily Dickinson we see all four modes developed, as we do also in Anna Akhmatova and Antonio Machado and Cesar Vallejo. Ai's poetry is a puzzle in this connection. She appears to be a thinking type who has not followed her natural path, but has allowed instead her feeling to take over the main function. What happens then is that the thinking becomes negative. Mephistopheles is the classic example; his repressed thinking doesn't think forward, but backward, and reduces all motives to greed. Ai's book *Cruelty* reduces all relationships to bodily hungers. Her thinking then is not undeveloped, but repressed, a process in which she actively cooperates. Her emphasis on cruelty is not original, but a compulsion in every person, man or woman, whose dominant function is repressed. We notice a similar emphasis on cruelty in a number of male writers, among them Clayton Eshleman and William Burroughs, who have elevated an unintegrated feeling side to kingship in the personality. Growth in these situations would seem to lie in restoring the thinking to its dominant place, and frankly admitting that the feeling is archaic and infantile, and trying to educate it, instead of leaning on it.

I'm not sure which mode is dominant in Galway Kinnell. I admire his poetry, but it's clear that he resolutely refuses to develop his thinking power; even in his finest poems he presents himself as a piece of feeling meat drifting through the universe. Evidently he does that out of some Roethke-like conviction, absorbed young, that the poet is a *feeler*. One of the helpful things about the four-mode vision is that it frees the poet from these initiatory tyrannies. The vision makes clear that a poet can have his or her grasp of physical fact dominant, or his feeling, or his thinking, or his intuitive intelligence. Great poetry can come no matter which one is dominant. The issue is how much the inferior one is developed. When the underneath power does begin, usually in the poet's thirties or forties to put out leaves and produce flowers, he or she experiences a sense of growth.

How much the inferior function gets developed is often a matter of will. During the last decades, when prevailing psychologies, both Western and Eastern, have dispraised and disrespected will, few people have developed their inferior function. All throughout the New Age culture we see gentle, will-less types, stagnant, stuck in their dominant function, which is usually feeling or intuition, checking the *I Ching* every day. Hard study or intense devotion to art is avoided, on the grounds that all such concentration is repressive. But will, as Neruda saw, is one of the few weapons we have in overcoming repression. Neruda wrote every day for two to three hours and supported political movements that emphasized the power of will. As a result, all four functions are remarkably developed in him. Feeling was dominant from the start, but his decision to run for senator in his thirties, and his intense studies of South American history, archeology, geology, marine life, and wildlife for *Canto General* were his ways of developing his grasp of facts. His other wing function, that of intuition, he saw was linked to Blake, whom he translated. His thinking was his weakest function, and remained so, but he worked on it constantly, even though he could never think his way out of Stalinism.

The new generation of poets such as Knott, Benedikt, Simic, Alta, Edson, Fraser, Strand, Tate, and Berrigan, to name only a few, have not shown much growth beyond their first books, and this may be linked to their reluctance to use will. A few may think they get permission from Eastern wisdom to "drift," but no poets show greater will than the Chinese poets, ancient or modern. All the American poets I've mentioned have also been typecast early on by critics, which means that the critics identify and praise them for their dominant power. The implication is that they published too early. Critics notoriously do not encourage development of the auxiliary powers, but prefer to categorize everyone by the function that first appears and then spend their time trying to get everyone to stay in his cubbyhole. Also this generation is too obedient. Edson has developed more of the functions, I'd guess, than anyone else, but much of his thinking is seductive, a little like Mephistopheles, and he feels trapped. Bill Knott has staggering powers of feeling and of intuition, but his obsession with the French surrealists is his way of avoiding the pain of developing a thinking function. The French surrealists are oddly naive in the matter of growth, and their doctrinaire tone shows how much repression they practice. Their repression (of the thinking function) is presented as freedom. But in a Breton poem it's clear that only intuition and a little feeling are present.

Former Defense Secretary McNamara is the classic instance of another kind of two-function man. His circle is turned so that the gap between thinking and grasp of worldly facts is on top. He had developed both intensely. He felt so much power in these that he steadfastly refused to develop his feeling side or his intuition alone, both of which remained stunted. As a result, he was responsible for the deaths of thousands in Asia, who probably had all four functions moderately well developed, as Buddhist country people generally do.

Americans tend to develop one function only, to be "one-sided," and noticing this should make the poets especially wary when they see this tendency in themselves. For example, in the last ten years most American poets have refused to put forward any theories about poetry. Often they say in interviews or contributors' statements that not having any theory makes them feel more like poets. Poetic theories, in fact, often spring to life whenever a writer tries to develop one of his or her weaker functions, and in fact, it is a mark of the effort. When William Carlos Williams says, "No ideas but in things!" you see an extrovert intuitive type—he was a good diagnostician—trying to develop his grasp of physical fact. He succeeded, and out of it came the contagious hospital poem, written from the function previously weakest, as many masterpieces are. When he remarks at the end of his poem about eating plums found in the icebox:

> They were delicious—
> so sweet and so cold.

We notice that he has written those lines with his previously weak sense mode, developed with so much will and energy. As he said in another famous little poem:

> so much depends
> upon
>
> the red wheel
> barrow
>
> glazed with rain
> water
>
> beside the white
> chickens.

I'd like those who love the poets I've mentioned here—I love many of them myself—to forgive this limited way of looking at them. An idea helps to see certain details sharply, but like a flashlight it leaves everything around them dark, and there is much more in the dark of each poet that I haven't mentioned.

1973

What the
Image Can Do

I

Poets my age and younger have probably placed too much emphasis on the image in recent years, too much, that is, in relation to the other powers of poetry, such as the dance of pitch, discourse, narrative, sound, and weight of thought. My own overemphasis on image has been partly at fault for that, but one could also say that other critics who should have balanced or corrected the overemphasis on image did not appear. I am glad of the new criticism by Robert Hass, Charles Molesworth, Frederick Turner, all practicing poets. The image brings so much moistness to a poem that it cannot, I think, be overpraised, but when a poet works on it solely or mainly he or she may, without intending it, let other beings in the poem starve. It's possible that Williams starved the resonating sound and thought areas of his poetry by working so doggedly on colloquial or spoken language.

The image belongs with the simile, the metaphor, and the analogy. Shelley said, "Metaphorical language marks the before unapprehended relations of things." Owen Barfield remarks in his marvelous book called *Poetic Diction* (which is about many other things as well) that he would like to alter only one detail in Shelley's sentence. He would change "before unapprehended relationships" to "forgotten relationships." He says that ancient man stood in the center of a wheel of rays coming to him from objects. As an example of a "forgotten relationship" we could mention the relationship between the woman's body and a tree. Medieval alchemists created drawings showing a woman taking a baby from a tree trunk. We all know other examples. Many relationships then have been forgotten—by us. They can be recovered. "For though they were never yet apprehended they were at one time seen," Barfield says. "And imagination can see them again." When a poet creates a true image, he is gaining knowledge; he is bringing up into consciousness a connection that has been forgotten, perhaps for centuries.

I think Barfield's understanding of the image is tremendous. The power of the image is the power of seeing resemblances. That discipline is essential to the growth of intelligence, to everyone's intelligence, but especially to a poet's intelligence. Emerson, who was Thoreau's master, said, talking of true analogies:

> It is easily seen that there is nothing lucky or capricious in these analogies, but that they are constant, and pervade nature. These are not the dreams of a few poets, here and there, but man is an analogist, and studies relations in all objects. He is placed in the center of beings, and a ray of relation passes from every other being to him.

The question then we have to ask of an image when we write it is, Does this image retrieve a forgotten relationship or is it merely a silly juxtaposition, which is amusing but nothing more?

II

Barfield maintains that every true image—every image that moves us—or moves the memory—contains a concealed analogical sequence. "Analogy" holds the word "logic" in it. He believes that the imagination calls on logic to help it create the true image and so to recover the forgotten relationship. He gives these lines of Shelley as text:

> *My soul is an enchanted boat,*
> *Which, like a sleeping swan, doth float*
> *Upon the silver waves of thy sweet singing.*

I'll try to work out the analogy implied. This is a possibility:

> *My soul is to your singing*
> *as a boat is to water.*

That's all right, but maybe a little bare.

> *My soul is to your sounds*
> *as a sleeping swan is to water.*

That sequence is better, because it includes the idea of enchantment, which has a secret resonance with "sleeping swan."

A great image contains logic, that is, thinking. One has to be intelligent to create an image and intelligent to understand it.

Two other lines Barfield quotes are more mysterious:

> *What is your substance, whereof are you made,*
> *That millions of strange shadows on you tend?*

We can feel enormous energy enter the poem with the word "millions." The energy is thought-energy that Shakespeare gave to the creation of the image. Barfield remarks that "sometimes in retracing the path back to the hidden analogy, a great deal of abstraction is necessary before we can arrive at the ratio." The ratio is his word for the sequence of analogies that we unravel slowly, but that the imagination saw in a flash as it was writing the poem. What is the hidden ratio that underlies Shakespeare's image? We can try this:

> *Your inner personality is to ordinary personality*
> *as a great magnet is to an ordinary stone.*

That's possible, but it doesn't feel quite right. Let's try this:

> *Your substance is to the mysterious interior being*
> *as a great medium is to ghosts longing to speak.*

That's better. Barfield however suggests this:

My experience of you is to the rest of my experience
as the sun is to the earth.

Delving like this makes clear that the true image has thought in it; complicated analogical, even logical, perceptions fuse with imagination to make a strong image.

It is particularly important at this moment to recognize the complicated power of the image in order to counter the disparagement of image that we find in critics who favor discourse. Many critics who defend discursive poetry—which I like as well—attack the image by maintaining that it often ignores intelligence. One young poet declared recently that the image denies "what can only be called intelligence, the possibility of reflection upon experience, the ability to make sense of our histories, our limits as well as our possibilities." Such a poet or critic may follow this attack with an image poem triumphantly made up in three minutes, as if composing images were easy, as if any high-school student could write images as well as Shakespeare or Trakl.

I like intelligence when it appears debating both sides of a question in the discursive poem, and I also like intelligence as it appears in an image. I would say that my respect for the image's power has deepened, rather than diminished, in the last few years.

III

Having called attention to Owen Barfield's praise of the logical thought underpinning a genuine image, I'll end this piece by making a distinction of my own between two sorts of images.

We know that the image merges worlds: Shakespeare with his "millions of strange shadows" joins the invisible world to the visible world. The true image has a room where each may live. An image may link the world of the dead with the world of the living. Trakl wrote,

> *The oaks turn green*
> *in such a ghostly way over the forgotten footsteps of*
> *   the dead.*

It may connect what we know with what we don't. Emily Dickinson wrote,

> *Exultation is the going*
> *Of the inland soul to sea—*
> *Past the houses, past the headlands,*
> *Into deep Eternity.*

It may join science and history. Blake said,

> *The Atoms of Democritus*
> *And Newton's Particles of light*
> *Are sands upon the Red Sea shore*
> *Where Israel's tents do shine so bright.*

Bert Meyers, a Los Angeles poet, writes about his days as a frame maker:

> *At dusk I drive home*
> *the proud cattle of my hands.*

The body let the cattle be its fatigue, and the spirit contributed its exultation.

These are all examples of the image as container. We don't need to be reminded that the alchemists had to create strong containers in order to fuse substances. We could say that the image fuses two sorts of consciousness in its strong container.

A second sort of image resembles a pole or an arrow more than a container. The image of this sort reaches out from human language to touch something else not entirely human. For example, if we imagine each sentence and each phrase in Blake's "Tyger" to point to a single power outside the poem, then the images that make up the poem are not so much containers as a verbal arm reaching out to touch the nonhuman.

> *What the hammer? what the chain?*
> *In what furnace was thy brain?*
> *What the anvil? what dread grasp*
> *Dare its deadly terrors grasp?*

The poem refers well beyond the animal.

The power of a myth depends on it embodying at least one of those "arm" images. An arm image, once found, can persist for centuries, passing from religion to religion, and worshippers never exhaust its possibilities. Yeats in one of his late poems has Mary say,

> *The terror of all terrors that I bore*
> *The Heavens in my womb.*

Yeats's image is an arm or a pole or a bridge. There is terror in the image because someone is approaching us over the bridge. We don't experience the bridge image as logical or analogical but as terrifying, numinous.

We remember that Hades in the myth of Persephone burst up from below, and Persephone either willingly, as the old texts have it, or unwillingly, as the later texts have it, went down with him. When searchers found the opening into the earth, her footprints were gone, obliterated by the footprints of pigs, for it turned out that a herd of pigs had gone down with the two. There is a terror in that image; and it reminds us of the pigs that Christ drove over a cliff.

Images of the bridge or arm sort carry us to conscious or superconscious matter. We feel that touching of superconscious matter in events that happen "synchronistically": after longing a whole week for a certain book we walk in a stranger's house and see it lying open on the table. Physicists who conducted the "Copenhagen experiments" found out that they could plot either the speed of a subatomic particle or its position. If the experimenter aimed to know its position, it would appear, but somehow it hadn't traveled there.

The bridge or arm images work against the notion that human intelligence is alone in the universe, isolated, and unchangeably remote from the natural world. Yeats's image reaches out with the left hand and touches a pregnant woman's conscious stomach and reaches out with the right and touches the superconscious "Heavens."

The Norwegians created an arm or pole image for Thor: lightning over a ripe barley field. Here the left hand touches the tips of the barley, and the right hand the superconscious energy they called "Thor." The ancient Gothic imagination was unwilling to accept the severe categorizations of inner and outer, divine and animal, intelligent and brute that Aristotle and later Descartes acquiesce in. This Gothic union, or oneness of worlds, is what Wallace Stevens suggests by the word "Harmonium." He stated his belief that sooner or later human beings will reappear who can grasp this doubly conscious world:

> And in their chant shall enter, voice by voice,
> The windy lake wherein their lord delights,
> The trees, like serafin, and echoing hills,
> That choir among themselves long afterward.

These images are wild, not domestic. Barfield says that the power that makes us able to touch "the Heavens" and the human skin at the same time is called "imagination." This large word has the smaller word "image" in it.

1981, 1989

A Playful Look
at Form

I

The word "form" when used about any creation suggests the idea of shape or body. It is natural to ask then: when we talk of form in poetry, does that mean an intellectual body or a sensual body? I think most critics of poetry imagine form as an intellectual structure, or a mental skeleton. When one follows that view one concludes that form adds something hard to the softness of feeling; it represents in small degree the eternal forms of which Plato speaks; it carries with it the clarity of the abstract or mathematical universe, the inexorable return of stars, the unemotional lines of geometry, the bony elegance of the triangle. I think there is much to be said for this concept of form, and I don't intend to dismiss it.

Donald Hall, however, has laid out a contrasting view of what poetic form is, what meter and rhyme at base are, and he puts form's essence elsewhere. His idea is that form in poetry involves three kinds of fun (which he calls sensualities), all linked to the earliest weeks of our life. The first is the baby's enjoyment of sounds, meaningless or not, which in the baby could be called mouth-fun or mouth-sensuality, and which in Milton becomes vast sonorities of vowels and consonants. The second sort of fun we see in the baby's kicking motions, especially when the baby is glad, and we could call that leg-fun or leg-sensuality, which continues as the adult's delight in dancing, and which informs those strong beats we notice in every line of Yeats. The third sort of fun is the infantile pleasure of appearance-disappearance. A baby sees its mother's face vanish, and loves to see it reappear again, and vanish and reappear. That is very like the way the sound in a rhymed poem disappears, and then suddenly reappears again at the very last moment. Such sensuality could be called in the baby the pleasures of peek-a-boo, or hiding and finding; and it becomes in adults the delight in rhyme and internal rhyme that we notice in every line of Marvell.

Donald Hall suggests that whenever we feel a given poem has "form," we are actually registering the presence of one or more of these forms of infantile fun. All three are easy to find in almost any Shakespearean sonnet. Here is mouth-sensuality or mouth-fun:

Bare ruined choirs, where late the sweet birds sang.

Here is the kicking fun or leg-stamping:

Th'expense of spirit in a waste of shame
Is lust in action, and till action, lust
Is perjured, murderous, bloody, full of blame,
Savage, extreme, rude, cruel, not to trust

The sense of dance comes in through the alternate accents, and in Shakespeare's case probably also in the
tune to which most of the sonnets were sung. Here is
the fun of peek-a-boo experienced in rhymes and half-
rhymes:

> Shall I compare thee to a summer's day?
> Thou art more lovely and more temperate;
> Rough winds do shake the darling buds of May,
> And summer's lease hath all too short a
> date . . .

In a Shakespeare sonnet the themes themselves perform
an appearance-disappearance drama in the closing couplet as well, to the great delight of the mind.

II

Hall gives a convincing demonstration that poetic
form, when looked at impishly or playfully, does not
relate itself only to adult discipline but to infantile pleasure as well. That assertion saws against the grain of a
lot of wood. Many a poet defending himself from
charges of doing nothing presents a picture of himself
alone wrestling manfully with his craft hour after hour.
His discipline in his craft is evidence surely of his serious
adult attitude toward life.

To cavort with Hall's idea a little further, let's assume
that the childlike and the infantile lie in the form; and
the adult contribution lies in the meaning or content.
Meaning and form then make two poles, across which
the magnetic energy of the poem arches. Certain cheer-

ful poets, whom I've called "hoppers," bring the infantile into the content, and then there's no place for the adult grief to go. Other poets, who call themselves formalists, imagine their iambic meter as a kind of militaristic correction of sixties sloppiness. When poets imagine form as adult, then meter becomes willed and mechanical; and what's worse there is no place now for the infantile spontaneity to go.

If, just for fun, we visualize the two poles of the poem in this new way—content as adult, form as childlike—we notice that they are opposite in charge, like the negative and positive poles of a battery. The cliché then that Charles Olson and many of his followers adopted, "Form is merely an extension of content," can be seen to be what it is—a ridiculous idea. It always was. Blake says that each artist needs the strength to endure the tension of fierce opposites. Blake's content is deeply adult, and his form deeply childlike and sensual. In his early poems particularly he is a child

> *Piping down the valleys wild,*
> *Piping songs of pleasant glee.*

Poets and scholars, Pound among them, have pointed out the immense metrical and rhyming ingenuity involved in the composition of the troubadour poems. We know now that the Spanish and French troubadours were influenced in that poetry by the sensuality of Arab civilization, particularly Sufi religious sensibility, carried by images of erotic love. The aura of erotic pleasure shines out from the language body of these troubadour poems, and the fun is there, while in the content certain ascetic ideas about "the love from far away" are being spoken.

III

There are two pulls. The playful form pulls the reader back toward infancy; the complicated meaning pulls the reader forward into adult states of mind. What happens when the poet places his or her most adult perceptions into the meaning? Then ascetic ideas (as in the Provençal poets) may come forward, compensating or contradicting the pleasure-loving language body; Heraclitean thought may come forward as in Machado, satire as in Quevedo, debate between Self and Soul as in Yeats, the praise of limits as in Olav Hauge or Transtromer. The adolescent is aware of early wants and early losses; the adult is aware of great causes and mythological beings. The adult poem then has "responsibilities" (in the Yeats view), or character, which we could term the ability to absorb joyfully experiences carrying pain—an ability or responsibility the infant never dreams of in his crib.

Following Whitman, most contemporary poets have gone directly on an express bus to free verse. In the free verse that we write, childlike or adolescent perceptions make up the content, and a childlike honesty provides the tone of the simple form. I have often tried myself, especially in the *Snowy Fields* poems, for this double clarity. There is no crime in such simplicity, but it can be a form of denial—a way to keep away from certain areas of adult experience.

Keeping the poem's content childlike is understandable. American poets feel themselves surrounded by a prematurely senile, rigid and stiff-legged culture, and so the garden of the poem they keep for their adolescent impulses and their spontaneous fantasies.

Russian poets have remained closer to the old poetic forms than we have, or perhaps they struggle more with them. Voznesensky's appearance-disappearance in assonance and rhyme is spectacular. At the same time his content is adult, open to the anguish of the Russian situation. Emily Dickinson is "Russian" in that she never read Whitman. H. D.'s poems are impressive, particularly in the way the vowels are made to recur. Gerard Manley Hopkins is a genius ten times over in his mouth-sensuality, his leg-fun, and his appearance-disappearance.

Our contemporary free verse is so busy being democratic, expansive, clear and sincere, direct to the gut, that we lose the troubadours and other pre-Whitman ancestors. We need the wise religious crone back in content, and the "wild old wicked man." How few poems in *The Best Poems of 1989*, a collection that I like, carry any hint of religious experience, neo-Platonic traditions, political agonies of choice, adult outrage, serious worship of Dionysius, debate on major issues. The Joseph Campbell interviews in his PBS series give a hint of what the wild old man and wise old crone content could be.

North American poetry in the last years continues to produce marvelous work from its best poets, poetry that is nourishing, lively, startling, and various; but in the matter of form-fun it is not so inventive. Playfully imaging complicated poetic form as infantile and childlike not only leaves a space open for adulthood in the content, but allows us to think of form in a less academic way. Hall's idea loosens up the concept of form. The idea has something in it of Dionysius, "The Loosener."

1974, 1989

Educating the Rider
and the Horse

I

I have been thinking lately that the poets of my generation have not been very faithful servants of art. What did Yeats say?

> *I know what wages beauty gives,*
> *How hard a life her servant lives,*
> *Yet praise the winters gone:*
> *There is not a fool can call me friend.*
> *And I may dine at journey's end*
> *With Landor and with Donne.*

We have been faithful and intense servants, but what we have served is the intensity of private material. Goethe said something like this: "In a work of art the private material is easiest to understand, the meaning more difficult, and the form still more difficult, and few can fathom it."

I imagine private material to be close to the chest, perhaps inside the chest; it needs the bone protection;

and I imagine meaning to be floating several feet out from the chest, between the chest and the human community. Meaning is a wild thing, passed to us through centuries by old men and old women, it is knowledge passed hand to hand, so to speak, and something secret comes with it. If we follow the metaphor, form then would live still farther out, still farther from the chest, and would be still wilder. That may be why it is more difficult to understand. This view comes as a surprise to me because I have often thought of form as a prison, a kind of dungeon in which heart material gets imprisoned. If I have been wrong on that, then I need to find a way to speak of form so that its wild or intense quality becomes clear.

II

In imagining form as wild, we don't get much help from the writers of standard texts on form. I. A. Richards comments in his *Principles of Literary Criticism:*

> *The whole conception of meter as "uniformity in variety," a kind of mental drill in which words, those erratic and varied things, do their best to behave as though they were all the same, with certain concessions, licenses and equivalences allowed, should nowadays be obsolete . . . though it has been knocked on the head vigorously enough by Professor Saintsbury and others, it is as difficult to kill as Punch.*

Paul Fussell, writing thirty years later, says,

Meter inheres in more or less regular linguistic rhythm; or we can say that talk about meter is a way of describing our awareness of those rhythmical patterns in poetic language which can be measured and formulated. Perhaps when we speak of meter we mean the "ideal" patterns which poetic rhythms approximate. That is, if meter is regarded as an ideal and thus invariable formal pattern, then rhythm moves toward meter the closer it approaches regularity and predictability. (Poetic Meter and Poetic Form)

C. S. Lewis in "Meter" says, "When we ask for the meter of a poem we are asking for the paradigm." W. K. Wimsatt, Jr., and Monroe Beardsley, in "The Concept of Meter: An Exercise in Abstraction" declare that "meter is something which for the most part inheres in language precisely at that level of linguistic organization which grammars and dictionaries and elementary rhetoric can successfully cope with."

Most critics then, as I. A. Richards complains, use the mechanical model when they talk of form, and omit what we could call the organic model. The mechanical model is taken from human economy, and the other from the economy of nature. We could easily oversimplify the distinction, but we'll stick with it a few minutes. The mechanical model—a predictable paradigm, for example—depends on certain mechanical repetitions human beings have achieved, in clocks and other geared machines, in belted factories and so on. The second or organic form draws from the success nature has had in its plant and animal adaptation. It is the second form that would deserve the term "wild" because the word "wild" refers to what humans have not domesticated, what is still receiving nourishment from nature.

III

A living animal's body reconciles various energies. We note that "form" is close to "shape," and both words suggest a body that holds in balance certain energies, even conflicting energies, as a snail shell reconciles both circular and linear drives. A good body does not destroy the energies or allow them to destroy the body. Wallace Stevens said, "I placed a jar in Tennessee." A shape is a container, but it also implies order, for example, a beginning, middle, and end, something that chaos does not have. A snail shell certainly has a beginning, middle, and end. We notice that form implies some sort of return. We say the universe has form because the Dog Star returns, the moon returns to full each month, spring returns each year, the salmon return to their rivers. In the snail shell, a certain curve, which can easily be plotted, returns everywhere in the shell.

As primitive animals move toward the mammal form, their adaption becomes more complicated, and attention is paid to breathing, speed of the heart, heat of the blood. Speed of heartbeat seems associated with the successful adaptation that hummingbirds have made. In the tiger, its interior bone structure, the heartbeat, the lungs, the sinews in legs and neck help it to be a shape that contains fierce energies, and helps it to survive among other fierce energies. By contrast, if we imagine a poem composed in mechanical form, correctly paradigmatic—a villanelle for example—as an animal, it would appear rigid, stiff-kneed, with medieval coloring, and so poorly adapted to the ground and trees around it that it would not survive the winter.

If we imagine one of Whitman's long poems as an animal, it would be an animal about a mile and a half long with not enough bone structure between head and tail, big in the stomach, and so cumbersome it would be killed by the first lion that noticed it on the grassy plain.

The animal that survives in the wild, the tiger, the horse, the wolverine, has just the right number of bones, just the right number of feet, a good balance of lung and heart, and just the right number of vertebrae. Moreover, it somehow fits the continent on which it lives.

So when we speak of form as a wildness and consider a poem's form as drawn from the careful economy of nature, we imagine the wild poem as an animal that moves fast, can leap in the air, escape from professors or metricists, and live for generations, even during the leanest climatic times.

I maintain then that the more form a poem has—I mean living form—the closer it comes to the wild animal.

Supposing that were true, what helps nudge the poem toward gazelle form or wolf form? First, passionate speech. Yeats said, "I love all the arts that can still remind me of their origin among the common people, and my ears are only comfortable when the singer sings as if mere speech had taken fire . . ." If we mumble, and apologize for speaking, we are victims; the lion is not a victim. Rumi says, "You're always most handsome when you're looking for food."

Second, "sentence sound." It is a certain sequence of pitches. Frost describes it this way:

You recognize the sentence sound in this: You, you . . . !
It is so strong that if you hear it as I do you have to
pronounce the two yous differently. Just so many sentence
sounds belong to man as just so many vocal runs belong
to one kind of bird. We come into the world with them
and create none of them. What we feel as creation is only
selection and grouping. We summon them from Heaven
knows where under excitement with the audile imagi-
nation. And unless we are in an imaginative mood it is
no use trying to make them, they will not rise. We can
only write the dreary kind of grammatical prose known
as professional.

This, Frost said, is "the most important thing I know."

Third, the conscious intensity—not sequence—of pitches. Syllables that rose high, very high, in the old Norse line the poets called "lifters." We can hear them in *Beowulf*. Sometimes the lifters resemble the peak of a roof, sometimes the dragon prow of a Viking ship that rises and falls. Sounds pronounced naturally in the roof of the mouth, such as "ee," drive the sound up; con-viction drives it up; the beat as it arrives helps drive it up. This is mysterious, unquantifiable.

Fourth, the animal rhythm that arrives over and above the human rhythm laid down. Milton in some passages of "Paradise Lost" provides a domestic rhythm of five beats, a kind of walking. His ear can hear over that a rhythm riding on three of those beats, which resembles a man running. Over that his ear can hear a third rhythm laid down on only two of those beats; and that third rhythm gives the feeling of an animal running. The three rhythms running together are too complicated to be paradigms, and our language is not subtle enough to describe them.

Finally, recurrence of vowel and consonant. Anglo-Saxon poetry creates much of its wildness in this way. A study of the way the Norse and Anglo-Saxon poets achieved this is too elaborate to be summed up. But one can say that when a sound is repeated in a certain way, the sound becomes alive and runs away.

IV

Talking this way we reach the threshold between domestic and wild form. On the threshold we are neither in the house nor out, neither in the conscious nor the unconscious, neither in this world nor the other world. That is where living form takes the poem. And thresholds belong to all betwixt and between places, to the heron that is neither land bird nor sea bird, to mercury that is neither metal nor liquid.

Ancient Celtic women would sometimes lay hard conditions on a man courting them. Conflicting loyalties and obligations often made serious courting dangerous for both parties. Moreover no woman wants to offer "the friendship of her upper thighs" to a man who can't solve riddles, or is too straitlaced, or has no playfulness in his soul. So she might say, you can come to me, but neither in the day nor the night, and neither riding nor walking, and you should be neither in the house nor out.

The wise lover might appear at her door then lying

across a short pony, with his legs dragging, so he is neither riding nor walking, at dusk, which is neither day nor night; and once he arrived at her door he wouldn't call to her until the pony's front legs were inside the house and the back legs outside. Once he had fulfilled all conditions, they could do what they wished, because they were neither in this world nor the next.

V

Loving meaning in the way Goethe speaks of means investigating the mythological implications of images in the way Goethe or Yeats actually did. Investigating images and their meaning is education of the rider. Studying how drummers catch fire is educating the horse. Drummers as we know do not aim for the rigid or mechanical paradigm that Fussel and Wimsatt praise as form. There is a place on the threshold then that educates both rider and horse.

When we are on the threshold, we can begin to imagine or reimagine for poetry a form neither reimposed nor free, which arrives at the betwixt time, neither night nor day, neither walking nor riding, and the poetry would be neither inside the house nor out.

1981, 1989

EPILOGUE

Knots

of Wild Energy

An Interview with Wayne Dodd

DODD: I see a curious contradiction in contemporary poetry. On the one hand, there is the most incredible amount of poetic activity going on. On the other hand, there is evidence of a real absence of sureness of direction and even purpose. This uncertainty is reflected even in such things as a call recently by a literary magazine for people to comment on what is to be the role of, say, form, or content, in poetry. It seemed to be symptomatic of a deep uncertainty. I wonder what would be a way of trying to make sense of that. Maybe you could talk about, for example, what the generation of poets under thirty-five show us, in their work, that would comment on this.

BLY: I think I feel the same disquiet as you do. Twenty years ago there may have been fifteen books of poetry published every year. Now, there may be sixty or seventy. They are published by the commercial presses, by the university presses like Pitt, and maybe another hundred or two hundred by small presses. I think the directory of poets includes four or five hundred poets now. It's an extremely new situation, because poetry in this country has always been associated with what could be called knots of wild energy, scattered at different places throughout the country. In the fifties there were only a few visible: William Carlos Williams, E. E. Cummings, Richard Eberhart, Kenneth Rexroth, Robinson Jeffers, Wallace Stevens, and Marianne Moore. They were geographically separate, and none were connected to universities. Ezra Pound and T. S. Eliot were in Europe. They represented self-creating and self-regulating knots of psychic energy. In fact, they resembled wild animals. Even though Wallace Stevens was working for an insurance agency, the part of him that wrote poetry was a wild animal.

It seems to me that what has taken place is the domestication of poetry. If you're going to follow that through, you're going to have to imagine the mink or the otter being brought into cages and bred there. Oftentimes, animals reproduce more in captivity because the young are not killed off. If you bring a species to optimum conditions, you have a vast supply of them in the next generation. But the new otters don't know the same things that their parents did. The original otter knew what cold water was like or knew how to live in the snow. That's one metaphor to explain the amazing tameness of the sixty to eighty volumes of poetry published each year, compared with the compacted energy of a book by Robinson Jeffers that appeared the same year as a book by Wallace Stevens, and those appearing the same year as one of Eliot's extremely kooky books.

DODD: Not only tameness, but sameness.

BLY: Sameness! It would follow somehow that someone is controlling the genetic breeding, and no new blood is coming in from the outside. So you have that sameness of the workshop. The workshops would be the breeding stations, I suppose.

I feel that the domestication is being done by two entities now: the universities, and the National Endowment for the Arts. When the government gives money, it results in domestication of the poet. I think that the National Endowment is an even worse catastrophe, in the long run, to the ecology of poetry than the universities. Talking yesterday to a class, I said, "Wayne understands the whole issue of the wildness that's involved with poetry, and how slowly animals in the wild learn to do things." You have grown slowly in poetry. So you're in a spot, actually, when you teach a workshop, because as you know, the funny thing about a workshop is that we want people to write fast, to write in their early twenties. That's impossible! They even want to get a job with it. How do you feel about that?

DODD: I agree entirely, and even though I make my living doing this, I always feel uncomfortable with a workshop situation because it seems to me to be such an essentially negative, or to borrow your metaphor, domesticating, function. Understandably, anyone

working in a workshop situation, let's say on a continuing basis in a writing program, who feels as though
he is learning to write, is going to feel that he is being
taught to do something: that he's being taught how to
write a poem. The things that will happen to him and
to others he will see working in the workshop, are the
things that will finally become in his mind the paradigm
for how to make poems. And yet, my own perception
is that, unless we're awfully careful, that doesn't teach
you to write poems. Often it teaches you how *not* to do
certain things. It teaches you how not to make gross
mistakes that are going to be unacceptable.

BLY: Ah, yes! Go on, give me an example.

DODD: The image I have is that a person brings in a
poem, and it has some good stuff in it but also has a
bunch of bad, which everyone with some sophistication
perceives as bad. You know, maybe it ends wrong. So
the teacher immediately hits that poet on the nose with
a newspaper and says, "Not here! Outside!" and so
teaches him not to pee on the rug in the house. After
a while he learns not to do that. He learns how to write
poems without those mistakes in them. But is that the
same as learning to write poetry? What I worry about
is not getting the positive aspects of poetry in there. As
you put it, "The growing into a sense of what's inside."

BLY: The poet bringing in a shallow ending to a poem
can be taught not to do that. What you're saying is that
we have poets who learn in the workshops not to make
disastrous mistakes. But then what?

DODD: Another metaphor I use sometimes is that real poems have navels; you can always find a navel in a poem.

BLY: What is the navel? Do you mean, for example, the connection between Maude Gonne and Yeats through which the poem somehow flows?

DODD: No, I don't think so. I'm thinking of the sense of human imperfection, of the profoundly real divisions and tensions in the psyche, of the individual depth of human experience. That is still, in itself, rather wild.

BLY: I can hear a typical workshop poet say to you: "What do you mean? I wrote a poem on my grandfather last year and I made it very clear he went through certain experiences cutting wood or farming that I haven't. Now my admission is tension and it is anguish, it is a navel." What do you say to that?

DODD: I think that the poem that we're talking about at the moment is the poem that, finally, lacks content. I think the only content of a poem is the positive or true emotional life of the individual.

BLY: Then he or she might say, "You're being insulting to me. I am twenty-three years old. I have a true emotional life. What right do you have to say that I don't have one?"
Who can answer that? But I know talking to you that I am not talking with a twenty-four year old. You have been working in poetry for fifteen to twenty years, and your poetry has grown slowly stronger and stronger.

You know how long it took you to arrive at the place where you are. Don't you find a contradiction between your experience and the expectation of the workshop student, who expects that within two years, if he studies with you, he will have a manuscript acceptable enough to get an MFA, and possibly get published? How do you deal with that contradiction?

DODD: I deal with it by agreeing with you and saying I accept it. I try to tell students about it. Anyone who comes into a program thinking he's going to learn short-cuts is doomed to failure. There is no such thing as a shortcut. I think that one can learn certain skills, certain devices, and maybe indeed speed up the process of learning poetry somewhat. But there are no real short-cuts.

BLY: But they're still winning. They're winning because they're receiving the knowledge that you have received in fifteen years of writing poetry, and you are giving it to them and they are accepting it. Both of you have the tacit understanding that out of it will come a manuscript acceptable for an MFA and possibly for a published book. So actually, even though you are warning the students about it, they are still winning and taking what they want and you are giving it to them.

DODD: I certainly think that that is the case with many writing schools in this country.

BLY: I'm in the same situation. If I come into a college, even for one day, I can find no reason for not teaching what I know. But I'm still going along with the unreality of the student, who imagines that by listening to an older poet for a while, he or she will be able to substantially improve the manuscript, so it will be more likely to be published. This ignores everything that the *Tao-te-ching* talks about, in terms of the slow flow of human life, the slow growth of oak trees, and all of that. There's some kind of lie that the workshops, and visiting poets, are involved in. I'm involved in it.

DODD: Don't you think that the real problem lies somehow outside the expectations of the student? I think their expectations *are* a problem, but perhaps there is a real problem also in the response of—I don't know what we're going to call it—the keepers of the system and the tradition, in their accepting and reinforcing that expectation.

BLY: Who are the keepers of the system?

DODD: Well, I suppose book publishers and editors.

BLY: It is a responsibility of publishers not to publish so many books of poetry. But you know what's happened. With the National Endowment supporting presses, a young man or woman can start a press. The National Endowment does not pay him a salary, but he can use some of the money given him to pay at least for the secretarial work, which the wife or husband or friend may do in connection with a book. There's a lot of genial corruption going on in that area. Books get published without risk or sacrifice—that's a book that shouldn't be published. That may sound stupid. I hear people say that the more books of poetry published the better. I don't agree. First of all, one often notices that poets who publish a book early often end up repeating themselves later on. Readers want to be amused. If you do something well—and we all know poets who have done that early on—the readers constantly urge the poet to do the same thing over again. By thirty-five he hasn't grown a bit. If he hadn't published early, but waited till his thirties, then, like Wallace Stevens or Walt Whitman, both of whom didn't publish until their late thirties and early forties, more growth would have taken place before *and* after that time. It seems to me that workshops are extremely destructive in the way they prepare students for publishing ten years too early.

DODD: You would agree, then, that that system is a system of avoidance of pain? It seems to me that's the exact opposite way of going about discovering how to write profound poetry.

BLY: That's very interesting, because the best part of workshops, probably, is the pain that a writer feels when someone criticizes his poem in public. But it hadn't occurred to me that this may be a substitute for the long-range pain that a person working alone feels, when he feels despair looking at his manuscript, knowing it is inadequate.

I've had that experience so many times. I'd prepare a group of two dozen poems, in my twenties, type them up excitedly, and then discover I had only two or three poems. Then I would fall into a depression for several weeks. After a few months I would put together another group of twenty, and this time find again in despair that maybe five were genuine. This solitary pain, with no one to relieve it, is a typical situation of the wild animal writer. The workshops take away some of that pain by having someone there to encourage you. Your friends in the workshop encourage you; "This is better than your last poem. I'd publish it." And I guess that amounts to an avoidance of pain.

I found out recently that one of the stronger labors in my life has been the labor to avoid unpleasant emotions. Pain is probably one of those.

DODD: I worry too about the writer's perception of what a poem is. I worry that the person will come genuinely to believe, as he's working on and living with a poem, that doing certain things is equivalent to the poem itself and to the basic instinct or impulse to poetry. I worry about the possible insinuation of a kind of "imitation" as the essential gesture of poetry. What do you think?

BLY: Let's go back to the image of domestication. In the wild state males fight each other. One of the things that has disappeared in the last twenty years in poetry has been the conflict between the young man and the old one. And the progress of the generations does not move well in any field unless the younger scientists or poets are willing to attack the older ones. Ortega y Gasset describes the process clearly in *Meditations on Quixote*. He begins four or five generations before Galileo. Astronomers then loved their teachers. But the young astronomers worked hard to find the flaw in their teacher's work. Each generation by that labor overturned the one before. This constant thought movement finally led to the astounding achievements of Galileo. Ortega makes it clear that in a healthy situation that is how males behave.

I participated in that a little when I started *The Fifties*. I started the magazine precisely to attack Allen Tate's and Robert Penn Warren's view of poetry. The reason for that is not because I hated Allen Tate. As you remember, in the fifties the shade from Eliot and Pound and Tate and William Carlos Williams was a heavy shade. It was necessary to clear some ground, so there'd be a place for new pine trees to grow. That clearing is not being done now. Perhaps my generation is casting shade now. The younger poets are not attacking Galway enough, or Merwin, or Wright, or Creeley, or Ginsberg. They're a little slow in attacking me, too. The women don't attack Levertov or Rich. The younger poets are being nice boys and girls. Partly it is cultural, the sixties' obsession with good feeling. But the normal process of human growth from generation to generation involves, as Ortega details, the new generation attacking the older one. And attacking them strongly, wiping them out as far as possible.

DODD: Just as Eliot did when he attacked Browning.

BLY: Oh yes; Eliot's work seems a new thing to us, invented, but Eliot's old man was Browning. And Eliot, by using allusions where Browning used a standard, straightforward continuity of detail, actually was attacking and overturning Browning's dramatic monologue, and it was so felt at the time. All the Browning people thought *The Waste Land* was absolutely disgusting. *Time* magazine called it a hoax. Eliot was pointing out that Browning was boring in the way he strings his perceptions of human beings together with no empty place for our imagination to enter. So Eliot decided to do a different portrait—for example, the portrait of his wife in *The Waste Land*, and he left big gaps in the portrait. In fact, he just left out entire arms and legs. *The Waste Land* is an attack on Browning and a victory over him. Eliot also did a lot of attacking in criticism; he was a very serious critic. This struggle is related to a fact about male animals Konrad Lorenz discovered. In the wild, two males, let's say pheasant cocks, spend some weeks in the spring settling the issue of territory. Perhaps a rooster will want a quarter of a mile. The defeated male retires from the territory. When the fights are over, the rooster who remains accepts the first female who enters the territory. Essentially he has cleared ground so that there will be enough for himself, the hen, and the chicks to eat. The stag fights are similar. A stag may need five or ten square miles, but the only way to ensure enough space is for the males to fight. No one understood that before. People in the nineteenth century thought that stags were fighting over the females, but actually they're fighting over the space. My metaphor then is that the younger poets, in failing to attack Merwin, or Rich, or Levertov, or me, or Ginsberg, or Simpson, or Hall, or Ed Dorn, are not doing their job. They are not making a place for their chicks.

DODD: You mean, of course, they are not attacking them in criticism and reviews. But you mean in their work too? That they're not attacking them there also?

BLY: I think it's mainly the absence of public criticism that's a disaster: the disappearance of criticism. Private criticism doesn't count. We notice magazines with nothing but poems in them, not a single review or "idea" article. The cliché of the last ten years is, "I want to say something positive. If I can't say something positive I don't want to say anything at all." There is a fear of having and using power. Imagine a stag in the north woods saying, "Well, I want to like all the other stags. I don't want any power. So I'll just take my horns off." To me one of the disasters that's happened is that so many poets have gotten the habit of emphasizing their own work, and have been unwilling to face head-on the poetry of others, older or even their own age. Ashbery is an example, Berrigan, Wakowski, Dubie, Gluck, Ginsberg. Many poets at poetry readings read nothing but their own work.

The point is not that Eliot disliked Browning; he never met Browning. It was an attack of psychic energy only. But think of this situation by contrast: the medium generation of poets, Donald Justice, Marvin Bell, Dick Hugo, and so forth, are teaching in a college. The younger poets are grateful to poets like Justice and Bell for teaching them. This gratefulness to the older poet prevents them from doing the natural thing, which is to take the work seriously, turn on poets in the older generation, and attack them. Justice and Bell and Hugo don't want to be attacked, and they encourage the good feeling.

I was thinking of this only yesterday: that the university system, which seems in the beginning so sweet, where one can go in as a younger poet and find an older poet whom you admire to work with, causes everything to break down. We're living in a swamp of mediocrity, poetry of the Okefenokee, in which a hundred and fifty mediocre books—and they're mediocre partly because the men writing them are somehow not completely males, because they haven't broken through to their own psychic ground—are published every year. When a man or woman succeeds in grasping what his or her master has done, and breaking through it, he doesn't create something artificial. He enters through his belly button into the interior space inside himself. And there, to everyone's surprise, are new kinds of grass, and new kinds of trees, and all of that!

DODD: So that suddenly makes the term "tame" a real, living metaphor.

BLY: And it explains why, although it was so good in a way to get rid of the New Criticism—New Criticism, by the way, was itself a tiger, and John Crowe Ransom was Captain Carpenter. They attacked the life work of the historical critics with ferocity, and evicted it from the English departments. Then the *Kenyon Review* started to get a little pesty, but no one killed it, it just died. Maybe English departments believe in eternity. The result, I find, is a tameness and smugness in many younger male poets, the young female poets are tame also, and there is a tameness in criticism. Oftentimes I'll open a poetry magazine and there will be seventy pages of poetry and not one article. I hear poets who are proud never to have written criticism. They warble: "I'm very sensitive, you know. I'm a special person. Criticism should be done by corrupt types like university professors and journalists. I just love poetry."

There's one stupid magazine out in California. Do you

remember that one—*Poetry* . . . ? It's published in a format like *APR*.

DODD: Oh yes. *Poetry Now*.

BLY: Yes! A really stupid one! This magazine says, "I'm going to publish a review now of a book." And the book review consists of the title of the book, the name of the author, and one or two of the poems. And *APR* doesn't really have much criticism. It's edited by committee, and they specialize in thirty-page articles on Ashbery that no one can finish.

DODD: That's absolutely true, and that's a complaint that has been voiced by a lot of serious poets and critics lately. Donald Hall wrote recently about the need for real criticism. And Marvin Bell also once said, commenting on some negative criticism I had written of a book, that it was really important for us to keep writing criticism, and to keep reviewing. I was glad to hear Marvin say that.

BLY: I think it's a good idea for each poet to take a vow to review, let's say, two books every six months. It's a part of his discipline. And he doesn't wait to be assigned a review. He writes it and then finds a place for it later.

When my own generation began to write, around 1954–1958 or so, poetry and the persona were considered linked, and both were considered a child of the iambic rhythm. Allen Ginsberg, following Whitman, attacked those linkages by talking about his own life in *Howl*. And Jim Wright altered the relation of the iambic line to English poetry by bringing in whole areas of things that Keats had never thought about in relation to grief among the coal miners. And when he brought the slag heaps in, he found, following Trakl, that some new kind of consciousness in the twentieth century passes to the reader through the precise image, conscious and unconscious. Ginsberg uses mainly the mental or general image. I studied the precise image a great deal too. But we must see that the image is not a final solution. Many young poets are still writing calmly, almost smugly, in the image, without looking around. Obsession with image can become a psychic habit as much as obsession with persona, and we need new ways of bringing forward consciousness. Some hints have appeared, but few younger poets have cleared ground for themselves in that area. They have simply accepted the whole discovery of the image as it comes through, through Neruda, through Trakl, and the Americans.

And you could also say that this shows that the American male is solving his father problem less and less. It's quite possible that a hundred years ago there was much more resentment of the son against the father. The father after all controlled the keys to the economy, particularly if he were a master and you were the apprentice. Now the son can avoid living the whole father problem by going into a completely different field, say, computers. Maybe he doesn't realize that he still has to confront the father in some way. I think this failure in the artistic world is a reflection of a desire of the young males to live in a state of comfort, as opposed to the terrific state of tension and anger with your father which was more the situation a few generations ago.

DODD: Speaking of criticism, it seems to me that one sees a resurgence, or upsurge, or something like that, in the last few years, of what I would call the "new neoclassicism."

BLY: All right, give me an example.

DODD: I'm thinking of the criticism written by Harold Bloom, and poetry by people such as Ammons and Ashbery.

BLY: And in what sense is that neoclassic?

DODD: Well, I think the way in which it emphasizes strictly formal and intellectual concerns and almost wholly denies the emotional.

BLY: Ashbery would say that his poetry is actually rather surrealistic. So how can you reconcile those two adjectives?

DODD: Ashbery is surrealistic at times, that's true. But I find very little emotion. I find that his surrealism much of the time is not getting at other, more disturbing realities, but keeping away from them.

BLY: I follow what you're saying, because if you examine something like *Beowulf*, it's perfectly clear that neither the poet nor the reader can go on eighty lines without going into a powerful gut feeling like deep thankfulness, or anger. One can go through pages of Ashbery and never find any emotions beyond those that the cerebellum is capable of. Neoclassic critics are writing again, suggesting that perhaps Yvor Winters was right, after all. Robert Pinsky is one.

DODD: And I'm thinking of Pinsky too.

BLY: Are you? The old dualistic line doesn't change, it seems, no matter what else changes. The Yvor Winters types just remain. They are like the old VW Beetle and remain the same from generation to generation. But the academies have also produced a new sort of academic critic, and Bloom surely belongs to them.

DODD: An odd thing about Bloom's criticism is that it consists of "forwarding" a poet.

BLY: That's interesting. It hasn't always been that way. Samuel Johnson was a critic who was willing to tackle even Shakespeare. He'll say this scene with Cordelia is absolutely absurd, or he'll declare about a certain passage, "I'm sorry to say that human beings do not speak this way." In most cases he's right. A critic's task is to find where genuine feeling is not touching the words, or not nourishing the words, and so point out the fake areas so that others become aware of the problem. Mencken did that, constantly, with every speech a president gave. Edmund Wilson did it with novels. You can't appreciate the great unless you see where it fails. But Harold Bloom decides to "creatively" uplift his subjects, so instead of criticizing what is there in the shadowy area, being uncomfortable, he elevates Ashbery and Ammons, a very unusual thing for a critic to do. What he is elevating upward is some kind of a . . . , well, I suppose to go back to your image, it's poets that know precisely how not to pee on the rug. They never do that; they're very well mannered. They ostensibly have a shirttail relation to Wallace Stevens. But they do not have the grandeur of Stevens. Ashbery has become an utterly academic poet. Academic poetry in the fifties was recognizable by emotional anemia and English meter. Now it is recognizable by fake French surrealism and emotional anemia. In Ashbery there is no anger, there is no world. There are no trees, there are no animals, there are no women; there is no oppression, there are no dictators; there's actually no intense compassion! There are no characters as in Chaucer. You have an academic anemia disguised as the French avant-garde and almost none of the critics, young or old, have the guts to see through it. Ashbery has a kind of genius. But I also feel that his poetry is empty and academic.

DODD: What about the use of the unconscious in American poetry today? For a time, after the work you and others did in the fifties and sixties, breaking down a parochialism of the imagination, it seemed that a good many poets were beginning to respond to this in their work. But now I see poems in which the signs ought to be pointing in that direction, but there is no road into the power of the unconscious where the wild is, to go back and borrow your metaphor. Is this an example of what you were just saying about Ashbery, finding dodges to make it seem that one is doing one thing when in fact one isn't?

BLY: That's very interesting. D. H. Lawrence wrote of this progression, using the image of the umbrella. Kafka or Conrad, let's say, rips holes in the umbrella; then one sees through to the night sky and the stars, which in this case represent the unconscious. That's rather scary. Poe did that. What happens next? A Longfellow type appears; he makes another umbrella and this time paints stars on the inside of it. And grateful readers say, "Look at that sky! Look at the wonderful stars up there!" Andy Warhol does that in relation to what Max Ernst was doing. It may be that this sort of thing goes in waves. After all, some nonliterary Conrad in the psyche tore off the umbrella and showed Americans the Vietnam War. So the whole nation insists on comfortable stuff again. "Don't scare me." Writers who want to deal with the true unconscious will be alone for a while.

DODD: Do you think there is a kind of correspondence between the fact of, on the one hand, the presence of this domestication of the poet learning forms and formulas and, on the other hand, this academicism? Because academicism doesn't want the wildness anyway?

BLY: I went to the Iowa workshop a year ago. In general what was being taught was technique. That was because there had been with the New Critics a swing away from Whitman and William Carlos Williams back to using English models again. If you look at *New Poets of England and America*, published in 1958, you see most models are English. But during the sixties most workshops, graduate at least, stopped teaching iambic technique. Why don't the workshops then emphasize the deep content, the angers, the confrontations, that you find in Neruda or Yeats; the political content that you find in Brecht, and so on? Why aren't those being emphasized? Well, as you so wonderfully say with the image of the rolled newspaper, some form of behavioral training takes place instead. Students are taught to write, as David Ignatow says sarcastically, "the perfect poem."

We have never before faced what it's like in the culture when hundreds of people want to write poetry and want to be instructed in it. In the Middle Ages, in the Renaissance, there weren't that many people who wanted to be painters; but if they did they went to a studio and entered into a deep father-son relationship with a painter, privately, one-to-one in his workshop. Now we are trying to instruct hundreds of beginning poets in the universities. We don't know how to instruct in that area. We know how to instruct a hundred engineers, or a thousand computer technicians, but that knowledge doesn't help. If you read a history of Ch'an Buddhism, you'll notice that Buddhism faced the same problem. It began with just a few people, and later huge numbers of people wanted Buddhist instruction. Ch'an Buddhism does not involve doctrine; it involves the same kind of thing we're talking about, breaking through the ego and getting down to the unconscious, breaking through conventional attitudes and getting down to the real ones, breaking through your society face and getting down to your genuine face.

They learned how to do that. Their method doesn't resemble a workshop. They didn't teach politeness or the smooth surface. They didn't teach "the poetry of fans" as Neruda would say. The teacher wouldn't assign an exercise to be done at the desk for the following week, but his plan would involve something entirely outside the building. Perhaps a man might come in and say, "I want to learn something about Buddhism. I want to get my degree in Buddhism in a year and a half. What books shall I read? You want me to do meditation exercises now?" The monk would say, "No, I don't think so. You go out in the woods there, and build yourself a little house, and live there six months, and then come back and see me."

"What shall I do?"

"Oh, that's your business. I don't know; you do what you want to. Don't have any servants or anything like that. Get your own water and bake your own bread."

So the man is out there for six months all by himself, and he is in charge of his own body. Finally he comes back and says, "Okay, I've done it. I've built my house and I'm ready now. Will you give me instruction?"

"Oh no, I don't think so. Actually we need a meditation hut out there very bad. I think you had better build that."

"What do I build it out of?"

"Oh, stones. There're a lot stones on that hill there. You can use those stones and build a house up there."

"How long will it take me?"

"Oh, six or eight months. When you're done come see me."

He comes back and says, "Well, okay. I'm done now. I want my instruction in meditation."

"Well, you haven't been moving around very much. Probably a good thing you see a little land. Why don't you take a trip around China? Make about a six-month trip. I'm busy. You come back, see me in six months."

And if he's willing to go through all that—actually during all that he is *doing* something and getting away from his mental attitude—he has received instruction. The instruction throws him back on his own body. By making him do things he understands that art is not a matter of getting something from a teacher. Art is a matter of going into your own resources and building. You may even have shown the student that it's necessary to build a house out of stone.

We're doing the opposite. We allow people to come to a workshop and receive immediately what you, for example, have worked ten to fifteen years to learn yourself. A nineteen-year-old student comes to your office, and because our teaching is structured so, we offer him that material right away. We can't say that plan is wrong or right. We can only say the Buddhists learned not to teach that way.

I must say that if I were going to teach a workshop on a long-range basis I would try to introduce some method of that sort. I would refuse to meet with the students regularly; but they would have to live away from the campus, in the woods or desert. They wouldn't be able to get any instruction until they had earned it, by breaking dependencies, doing things for themselves. One might say to a student, "After you have your hut, translate twenty-five poems from a Rumanian poet."

"But I don't know Rumanian."

"Well then, that's your first job. You learn Rumanian, translate the twenty-five poems, and then come back to see me, and I'll tell you what I think about 'the deep image.' "

One learns a lot by translating a great poet. By that method, we get closer to the actual way that art was taught in the Renaissance. You might go to Rubens, for example, and say: "I would like to be your student. Would you teach me your philosophy of painting?" And he might say, "Well, there's a shoe missing down in the left-hand corner. Please paint it so it looks exactly like the other shoe. Don't talk, paint."

DODD: What do you suppose accounts for the almost total absence of this sort of attitude from the writers in our society?

BLY: This contrast between "doing," which is the ancient way of learning, and "studying," which we want to do, I think is connected to the difference between the working class, who are always doing, and the white-collar classes.

In the Midwest, most of our grandparents or great-grandparents came here as immigrants, if from Scandinavia, they belonged to the working classes. Virtually all Norwegians were working class in the nineteenth century. So most of the immigrants were working class. But, the next generation doesn't want to be that way; they want to go to college. They want to rise.

The phenomenon of the university-based poet I think is linked to this longing. Many grandsons and granddaughters of immigrants are proud to be MFAs because it proves that they're not working class.

DODD: You know, Gary Snyder said something not unrelated to that in an interview we recently published. The interviewer could hardly believe what he was hearing when Snyder said that if a person wanted to learn how to be a poet he ought to go find a person who could "do" something well, and learn how to do it with him. Find, for example, a good carpenter. Or find a good mechanic, and then just stick with him for a while! Live with him, hang around him. Watch him and help him work. Learn to do it, maybe for two or three years. The interviewer finally said to him, "Are we still talking about poetry?" And Snyder said, "Fuckin' A we're still talking about poetry. You learn how to *write poetry* by learning how to do anything really well and proper."

BLY: Beautiful!

DODD: So that's surely related to the kind of thing you're talking about.

BLY: Surely it's related to Thoreau's care in building his house in which he learned how to put together a chapter.

In Worcester, Massachusetts, community poetry readings have been going for eight or nine years now. They have a wonderfully serious duo there: Mike True and Franny Quinn. They began the reading in the downtown library, which isn't a university setting. The community comes. Young poets now are glad to come and read at the library. Meanwhile Franny has been setting up readings in four or five places on the outskirts of Worcester, city halls or senior citizens' places or bars.

A poet says, "You know, I've been around a lot; I'd like to read at the library." And Franny says, "We'd like that, but we'd like you to read at three of these places also." Well, you drive out to an old town hall at six o'clock on Friday evening, and there're four old men sitting there, and they've never heard a serious poem spoken in their life. So it's not a thrilling reading. There's no standing ovation. However, if you want to read at the library you do that too. So the poet says, okay. And the old men like to have young men come out and tell them about their marriages.

Then Mike or Franny might say, "That was fine. Now I'd like you to set up the program for the next group of poets we have coming through."

"What does that involve?"

"Well, it would mean going to, say, Lowell, and starting from scratch there to set up the reading places and dates."

"I can't..., ah, I'm not gonna..., I can't organ— ah, I'm not organizing... that's not..."

"Why not?"

"Well, I'm a poet."

"What does that mean?"

"Well, I'm just not an organizer. Some people do that well, really, but I just write poetry."

Then Franny might say, "I have one bit of news. I'm a poet and I've been organizing for eight and a half years, and you've just received the benefit of the organization. The job here would be to talk to the city council. Convince them the idea would work, ask for a spot, and so on, and do some work on the posters."

There's a great resistance to this, because being a poet with an MFA is a status symbol. Or even being "a poet" implies that in this country. So the resistance to crafting and learning by doing may go back to a fear of being working class.

DODD: What is the effect on poets of all the "sameness" you spoke of earlier?

BLY: Perhaps poetry is developing a protective camouflage of brown and gray feathers. A poetry shelf has fewer and fewer peacocks with long tails, like Robinson Jeffers. Probably this heavy breeding is nice. And it's possible that hawks don't see some gray birds and don't attack them, you know.

But if a person just beginning to read poetry walks into a bookstore and starts paging through all the boring gray and brown books of poetry, what does that do for the readership of poetry? When too much boring poetry is published, poets themselves begin to lose morale. I'm wondering how that could change.

I assume that the number of workshops will continue to increase. Then as the job offers go down, the new poets will become more and more tame, and more and more like the last generation. Suppose a number of poets would like a new position at Wisconsin, but Wisconsin wants to hire Galway Kinnell. That means that unconsciously, even consciously, the young poets will try to be more like Galway Kinnell. William Carlos Williams did not want to be like Galway Kinnell. Cummings or Marianne Moore did not have bureaucracy mentality. Each wanted to be wild separately! I don't see any possibility but its getting worse.

DODD: It may also be that poets will be afraid to risk doing the really different thing, that might seem to be profoundly true to them nonetheless, for fear of being accused of peeing on the floor.

BLY: Oh, indeed! That's right! I'm sure that the reviewers of Pound's early work, which had a lot of freaky originality, accused him constantly of being poorly house-trained. What would originality look like today? Perhaps it would involve intimate revelations not confessional, such as Akhmatova writes.

I don't believe originality will increase if the poetry becomes more primitive. Jerry Rothenberg to the contrary, most primitive poetry is probably boring. After you've said, "Here comes the otter, here comes the otter, here comes the otter. *A woka-woka-woka!* The bird flew down from the sky. Dawn is coming, *Wok-i-way*, I'm alive." You say that about ninety-eight times. . . . We live in an industrial society. I love the oral quality of primitive poetry, but how can a university be oral?

The problem is, how does poetry maintain itself as a vivid, highly colored, living thing? It's possible that originality comes when the man or woman disobeys the collective. The cause of tameness is fear. The collective says: "If you do your training well and become a nice boy or girl, we will love you." We want that. So a terrible fear comes. It is a fear that we will lose the love of the collective. I have felt it intensely. What the collective offers is not even love, that is what is so horrible, but a kind of absence of loneliness. Its companionship is ambiguous, like mother love.

Index

INDEX

Copyright Acknowledgments

Copyright Acknowledgments

Copyright Acknowledgments